ESSAYS IN
RADICAL EMPIRICISM

William James

DOVER PUBLICATIONS, INC.
Mineola, New York

Copyright

Bibliographical Note

This Dover edition, first published in 2003, is an unabridged and corrected republication of the work originally published by Longmans, Green, and Company, London, in 1912. We have reset the text; replaced the original French of essay VIII, "La Notion de Conscience," with a new English translation ("The Notion of Consciousness") by Stanley Appelbaum; made clarifications or other minor changes in most of the editor's footnotes; and completely repaginated the index.

Library of Congress Cataloging-in-Publication Data

James, William, 1842–1910.
  Essays in radical empiricism / William James.
    p. cm.
  Originally published: London ; New York : Longmans, Green and Co., 1912.
  Includes index.
  ISBN 0-486-43094-4 (pbk.)
  1. Experience. 2. Pragmatism. I. Title.

B945.J23E7 2003
146'.44—dc21

                                                    2003053261

Manufactured in the United States of America
Dover Publications, Inc., 31 East 2nd Street, Mineola, N.Y. 11501

EDITOR'S PREFACE

The present volume is an attempt to carry out a plan which William James is known to have formed several years before his death. In 1907 he collected reprints in an envelope which he inscribed with the title "Essays in Radical Empiricism"; and he also had duplicate sets of these reprints bound, under the same title, and deposited for the use of students in the general Harvard Library, and in the Philosophical Library in Emerson Hall.

Two years later Professor James published *The Meaning of Truth* and *A Pluralistic Universe,* and inserted in these volumes several of the articles which he had intended to use in the "Essays in Radical Empiricism." Whether he would nevertheless have carried out his original plan, had he lived, cannot be certainly known. Several facts, however, stand out very clearly. In the first place, the articles included in the original plan but omitted from his later volumes are indispensable to the understanding of his other writings. To these articles he repeatedly alludes. Thus, in *The Meaning of Truth* (p. 127), he says: "This statement is probably excessively obscure to any one who has not read my two articles 'Does Consciousness Exist?' and 'A World of Pure Experience.'" Other allusions have been indicated in the present text. In the second place, the articles originally brought together as "Essays in Radical Empiricism" form a connected whole. Not only were most of them written consecutively within a period of two years, but they contain numerous cross-references. In the third place, Professor James regarded "radical empiricism" as an *independent* doctrine. This he asserted expressly: "Let me say that there is no logical connection between pragmatism, as I understand it, and a doctrine which I have recently set forth as 'radical empiricism.' The latter stands on its own feet. One may entirely reject it and still be a pragmatist." (*Pragmatism*, 1907, Preface, p. ix.) Finally, Professor James came toward the end of his life to regard "radical empiricism" as more fundamental and more important than "pragmatism." In the Preface to *The Meaning of Truth* (1909), the author gives the following explanation of his desire to continue, and if possible conclude, the controversy over pragmatism: "I am interested in another doctrine in philosophy to which I give the name of radical empiricism, and it seems to me that the establishment of the pragmatist theory of truth is a step of first-rate importance in making radical empiricism prevail" (p. xii).

In preparing the present volume, the editor has therefore been governed by two motives. On the one hand, he has sought to preserve and make accessible certain important articles not to be found in Professor James's other books. This is true of Essays I, II, IV, V, VIII, IX, X, XI, and XII. On the other hand, he has sought to bring together in one volume a set of essays treating systematically of one independent, coherent, and fundamental doctrine. To this end it has seemed best to include three essays (III, VI, and VII), which, although included in the original plan, were afterwards reprinted elsewhere; and one essay, XII, not included in the original plan. Essays III, VI, and VII are indispensable to the consecutiveness of the series, and are so interwoven with the rest that it is necessary that the student should have them at hand for ready consultation. Essay XII throws an important light on the author's general "empiricism," and forms an important link between "radical empiricism" and the author's other doctrines.

In short, the present volume is designed not as a collection but rather as a treatise. It is intended that another volume shall be issued which shall contain papers having biographical or historical importance which have not yet been reprinted in book form. The present volume is intended not only for students of Professor James's philosophy, but for students of metaphysics and the theory of knowledge. It sets forth systematically and within brief compass the doctrine of "radical empiricism."

A word more may be in order concerning the general meaning of this doctrine. In the Preface to the *Will to Believe* (1898), Professor James gives the name *"radical empiricism"* to his "philosophic attitude," and adds the following explanation: "I say 'empiricism,' because it is contented to regard its most assured conclusions concerning matters of fact as hypotheses liable to modification in the course of future experience; and I say 'radical,' because it treats the doctrine of monism itself as an hypothesis, and, unlike so much of the halfway empiricism that is current under the name of positivism or agnosticism or scientific naturalism, it does not dogmatically affirm monism as something with which all experience has got to square" (pp. vii–viii). An "empiricism" of this description is a "philosophic attitude" or temper of mind rather than a doctrine, and characterizes all of Professor James's writings. It is set forth in Essay XII of the present volume.

In a narrower sense, "empiricism" is the method of resorting to *particular experiences* for the solution of philosophical problems. Rationalists are the men of principles, empiricists the men of facts. (*Some Problems of Philosophy,* p. 35; cf. also *ibid.,* p. 44; and *Pragmatism,* pp. 9, 51.) Or, "since principles are universals, and facts are particulars, perhaps the best way of characterizing the two tendencies is to say that rationalist thinking proceeds most willingly by going from wholes to parts, while empiricist thinking proceeds by going from parts to wholes." (*Some Problems of Philosophy,* p. 35; cf. also *ibid.,* p. 98; and *A Pluralistic Universe,* p. 7.) Again, empiricism "remands us to sensation." (*Op. cit.,* p. 264.) The "empiricist view" insists that, "as reality is created temporally day by day, concepts . . . can never fitly supersede perception. . . . The deeper features of reality are found only in perceptual experience." (*Some Problems of Philosophy,* pp. 100, 97.) Empiricism in this sense is as yet characteristic of Professor James's philosophy *as a whole.* It is not the distinctive and independent doctrine set forth in the present book.

The only summary of "radical empiricism" in this last and narrowest sense appears in the Preface to *The Meaning of Truth* (pp. xii–xiii); and it must be reprinted here as the key to the text that follows.[1]

"Radical empiricism consists (1) first of a postulate, (2) next of a statement of fact, (3) and finally of a generalized conclusion."

(1) "The postulate is that *the only things that shall be debatable among philosophers shall be things definable in terms drawn from experience.* (Things of an unexperience-able nature may exist ad libitum, but they form no part of the material for philosophic debate.)" This is "the principle of pure experience" as "a methodical postulate." (Cf. below, pp. 83, 127.) This postulate corresponds to the notion which the author repeatedly attributes to Shadworth Hodgson, the notion "that realities are only what they are 'known as.'" (*Pragmatism*, p. 50; *Varieties of Religious Experience*, p. 443; *The Meaning of Truth*, pp. 43, 118.) In this sense "radical empiricism" and pragmatism are closely allied. Indeed, if pragmatism be defined as the assertion that "the meaning of any proposition can always be brought down to some particular consequence in our future practical experience, . . . the point lying in the fact that the experience must be particular rather than in the fact that it must be active" (*Meaning of Truth*, p. 210); then pragmatism and the above postulate come to the same thing. The present book, however, consists not so much in the assertion of this postulate as in the *use* of it. And the method is successful in special applications by virtue of a certain "statement of fact" concerning relations.

(2) "The statement of fact is that *the relations between things, conjunctive as well as disjunctive, are just as much matters of direct particular experience, neither more so nor less so, than the things themselves.*" (Cf. also *A Pluralistic*

---

[1] The use of numerals and italics is introduced by the editor.

Universe, p. 280; *The Will to Believe,* p. 278.) This is the central doctrine of the present book. It distinguishes "radical empiricism" from the "ordinary empiricism" of Hume, J. S. Mill, etc., with which it is otherwise allied. (Cf. below, pp. 22–23.) It provides an empirical and relational version of "activity," and so distinguishes the author's voluntarism from a view with which it is easily confused—the view which upholds a pure or transcendent activity. (Cf. below, Essay VI.) It makes it possible to escape the vicious disjunctions that have thus far baffled philosophy: such disjunctions as those between consciousness and physical nature, between thought and its object, between one mind and another, and between one "thing" and another. These disjunctions need not be "overcome" by calling in any "extraneous trans-empirical connective support" (*Meaning of Truth,* Preface, p. xiii); they may now be *avoided* by regarding the dualities in question as only *differences of empirical relationship among common empirical terms.* The pragmatistic account of "meaning" and "truth," shows only how a vicious disjunction between "idea" and "object" may thus be avoided. The present volume not only presents pragmatism in this light; but adds similar accounts of the other dualities mentioned above.

Thus while pragmatism and radical empiricism do not differ essentially when regarded as *methods,* they are independent when regarded as doctrines. For it would be possible to hold the pragmatistic theory of "meaning" and "truth," without basing it on any fundamental theory of relations, and without extending such a theory of relations to residual philosophical problems; without, in short, holding either to the above "statement of fact," or to the following "generalized conclusion."

(3) "The generalized conclusion is that therefore *the parts of experience hold together from next to next by relations that are themselves parts of experience. The directly apprehended universe needs, in short, no extraneous trans-empirical connective support, but possesses in its own right a concatenated or continuous structure.*" When thus generalized,

"radical empiricism" is not only a theory of knowledge comprising pragmatism as a special chapter, but a metaphysic as well. It excludes "the hypothesis of trans-empirical reality" (cf. below, pp. 102–103). It is the author's most rigorous statement of his theory that reality is an "experience-continuum." (*Meaning of Truth,* p. 152; *A Pluralistic Universe,* Lect. V, VII.) It is that positive and constructive "empiricism" of which Professor James said: "Let empiricism once become associated with religion, as hitherto, through some strange misunderstanding, it has been associated with irreligion, and I believe that a new era of religion as well as of philosophy will be ready to begin." (*Op. cit.,* p. 314; cf. *ibid.,* Lect. VIII, *passim;* and *The Varieties of Religious Experience,* pp. 515–527.)

The editor desires to acknowledge his obligations to the periodicals from which these essays have been reprinted, and to the many friends of Professor James who have rendered valuable advice and assistance in the preparation of the present volume.

RALPH BARTON PERRY.

CAMBRIDGE, MASSACHUSETTS.
    January 8, 1912.

Contents

I.

DOES "CONSCIOUSNESS" EXIST?[1]

"Thoughts" and "things" are names for two sorts of object, which common sense will always find contrasted and will always practically oppose to each other. Philosophy, reflecting on the contrast, has varied in the past in her explanations of it, and may be expected to vary in the future. At first, "spirit and matter," "soul and body," stood for a pair of equipollent substances quite on a par in weight and interest. But one day Kant undermined the soul and brought in the transcendental ego, and ever since then the bipolar relation has been very much off its balance. The transcendental ego seems nowadays in rationalist quarters to stand for everything, in empiricist quarters for almost nothing. In the hands of such writers as Schuppe, Rehmke, Natorp, Münsterberg—at any rate in his earlier writings, Schubert-Soldern and others, the spiritual principle attenuates itself to a thoroughly ghostly condition, being only a name for the fact that the "content" of experience *is known.* It loses personal form and activity—these passing over to the content—and becomes a bare *Bewusstheit* or *Bewusstsein überhaupt,* of which in its own right absolutely nothing can be said.

I believe that "consciousness," when once it has evaporated to this estate of pure diaphaneity, is on the point of disappearing altogether. It is the name of a nonentity, and has no right to a place among first principles. Those who

---

[1] [Reprinted from the *Journal of Philosophy, Psychology and Scientific Methods,* vol. I, No. 18, September 1, 1904. For the relation between this essay and those which follow, cf. below, pp. 28–29. ED.]

still cling to it are clinging to a mere echo, the faint rumor
left behind by the disappearing "soul" upon the air of philosophy. During the past year, I have read a number of articles whose authors seemed just on the point of abandoning
the notion of consciousness,[2] and substituting for it that of
an absolute experience not due to two factors. But they
were not quite radical enough, not quite daring enough in
their negations. For twenty years past I have mistrusted
"consciousness" as an entity; for seven or eight years past I
have suggested its non-existence to my students, and tried
to give them its pragmatic equivalent in realities of experience. It seems to me that the hour is ripe for it to be openly
and universally discarded.

To deny plumply that "consciousness" exists seems so
absurd on the face of it—for undeniably "thoughts" do
exist—that I fear some readers will follow me no farther.
Let me then immediately explain that I mean only to deny
that the word stands for an entity, but to insist most
emphatically that it does stand for a function. There is, I
mean, no aboriginal stuff or quality of being,[3] contrasted
with that of which material objects are made, out of which
our thoughts of them are made; but there is a function in
experience which thoughts perform, and for the performance of which this quality of being is invoked. That function is *knowing*. "Consciousness" is supposed necessary to
explain the fact that things not only are, but get reported,
are known. Whoever blots out the notion of consciousness
from his list of first principles must still provide in some
way for that function's being carried on.

I

My thesis is that if we start with the supposition that
there is only one primal stuff or material in the world, a
stuff of which everything is composed, and if we call that

---

[2] Articles by Baldwin, Ward, Bawden, King, Alexander and others. Dr.
Perry is frankly over the border.

[3] [Similarly, there is no "activity of 'consciousness' as such." See essay VI
below, "The Experience of Activity," footnote 13. Ed.]

stuff "pure experience," then knowing can easily be explained as a particular sort of relation towards one another into which portions of pure experience may enter. The relation itself is a part of pure experience; one of its "terms" becomes the subject or bearer of the knowledge, the knower,[4] the other becomes the object known. This will need much explanation before it can be understood. The best way to get it understood is to contrast it with the alternative view; and for that we may take the recentest alternative, that in which the evaporation of the definite soul-substance has proceeded as far as it can go without being yet complete. If neo-Kantism has expelled earlier forms of dualism, we shall have expelled all forms if we are able to expel neo-Kantism in its turn.

For the thinkers I call neo-Kantian, the word consciousness today does no more than signalize the fact that experience is indefeasibly dualistic in structure. It means that not subject, not object, but object-plus-subject is the minimum that can actually be. The subject-object distinction meanwhile is entirely different from that between mind and matter, from that between body and soul. Souls were detachable, had separate destinies; things could happen to them. To consciousness as such nothing can happen, for, timeless itself, it is only a witness of happenings in time, in which it plays no part. It is, in a word, but the logical correlative of "content" in an Experience of which the peculiarity is that *fact comes to light* in it, that *awareness of content* takes place. Consciousness as such is entirely impersonal—"self" and its activities belong to the content. To say that I am self-conscious, or conscious of putting forth volition, means only that certain contents, for which "self" and "effort of will" are the names, are not without witness as they occur.

Thus, for these belated drinkers at the Kantian spring, we should have to admit consciousness as an "epistemolog-

---

[4] In my *Psychology* I have tried to show that we need no knower other than the "passing thought." [*Principles of Psychology,* vol. I, pp. 338 ff.]

ical" necessity, even if we had no direct evidence of its being there.

But in addition to this, we are supposed by almost every one to have an immediate consciousness of consciousness itself. When the world of outer fact ceases to be materially present, and we merely recall it in memory, or fancy it, the consciousness is believed to stand out and to be felt as a kind of impalpable inner flowing, which, once known in this sort of experience, may equally be detected in presentations of the outer world. "The moment we try to fix our attention upon consciousness and to see *what,* distinctly, it is," says a recent writer, "it seems to vanish. It seems as if we had before us a mere emptiness. When we try to introspect the sensation of blue, all we can see is the blue; the other element is as if it were diaphanous. Yet it *can* be distinguished, if we look attentively enough, and know that there is something to look for."[5] "Consciousness" (*Bewusstheit*), says another philosopher, "is inexplicable and hardly describable, yet all conscious experiences have this in common that what we call their content has this peculiar reference to a center for which 'self' is the name, in virtue of which reference alone the content is subjectively given, or appears. . . . While in this way consciousness, or reference to a self, is the only thing which distinguishes a conscious content from any sort of being that might be there with no one conscious of it, yet this only ground of the distinction defies all closer explanations. The existence of consciousness, although it is the fundamental fact of psychology, can indeed be laid down as certain, can be brought out by analysis, but can neither be defined nor deduced from anything but itself."[6]

"Can be brought out by analysis," this author says. This supposes that the consciousness is one element, moment, factor—call it what you like—of an experience of essentially dualistic inner constitution, from which, if you abstract the content, the consciousness will remain revealed to its own

---

[5] G. E. Moore: *Mind,* vol. XII, N. S., [1903], p. 450.
[6] Paul Natorp: *Einleitung in die Psychologie,* 1888, pp. 14, 112.

eye. Experience, at this rate, would be much like a paint of which the world pictures were made. Paint has a dual constitution, involving, as it does, a menstruum[7] (oil, size or what not) and a mass of content in the form of pigment suspended therein. We can get the pure menstruum by letting the pigment settle, and the pure pigment by pouring off the size or oil. We operate here by physical subtraction; and the usual view is, that by mental subtraction we can separate the two factors of experience in an analogous way—not isolating them entirely, but distinguishing them enough to know that they are two.

II

Now my contention is exactly the reverse of this. *Experience, I believe, has no such inner duplicity; and the separation of it into consciousness and content comes, not by way of subtraction, but by way of addition*—the addition, to a given concrete piece of it, of other sets of experiences, in connection with which severally its use or function may be of two different kinds. The paint will also serve here as an illustration. In a pot in a paint-shop, along with other paints, it serves in its entirety as so much saleable matter. Spread on a canvas, with other paints around it, it represents, on the contrary, a feature in a picture and performs a spiritual function. Just so, I maintain, does a given undivided portion of experience, taken in one context of associates, play the part of a knower, of a state of mind, of "consciousness"; while in a different context the same undivided bit of experience plays the part of a thing known, of an objective "content." In a word, in one group it figures as a thought, in another group as a thing. And, since it can figure in both groups simultaneously we have every right to speak of it as subjective and objective, both at once. The dualism connoted by such double-barrelled terms as "experience,"

---

[7] "Figuratively speaking, consciousness may be said to be the one universal solvent, or menstruum, in which the different concrete kinds of psychic acts and facts are contained, whether in concealed or in obvious form." G. T. Ladd: *Psychology, Descriptive and Explanatory,* 1894, p. 30.

"phenomenon," "datum," "*Vorfindung*"—terms which, in philosophy at any rate, tend more and more to replace the single-barrelled terms of "thought" and "thing"—that dualism, I say, is still preserved in this account, but reinterpreted, so that, instead of being mysterious and elusive, it becomes verifiable and concrete. It is an affair of relations, it falls outside, not inside, the single experience considered, and can always be particularized and defined.

The entering wedge for this more concrete way of understanding the dualism was fashioned by Locke when he made the word "idea" stand indifferently for thing and thought, and by Berkeley when he said that what common sense means by realities is exactly what the philosopher means by ideas. Neither Locke nor Berkeley thought his truth out into perfect clearness, but it seems to me that the conception I am defending does little more than consistently carry out the "pragmatic" method which they were the first to use.

If the reader will take his own experiences, he will see what I mean. Let him begin with a perceptual experience, the "presentation," so called, of a physical object, his actual field of vision, the room he sits in, with the book he is reading as its center; and let him for the present treat this complex object in the common-sense way as being "really" what it seems to be, namely, a collection of physical things cut out from an environing world of other physical things with which these physical things have actual or potential relations. Now at the same time it is just *those self-same things* which his mind, as we say, perceives; and the whole philosophy of perception from Democritus's time downwards has just been one long wrangle over the paradox that what is evidently one reality should be in two places at once, both in outer space and in a person's mind. "Representative" theories of perception avoid the logical paradox, but on the other hand they violate the reader's sense of life, which knows no intervening mental image but seems to see the room and the book immediately just as they physically exist.

The puzzle of how the one identical room can be in two places is at bottom just the puzzle of how one identical point

can be on two lines. It can, if it be situated at their intersection; and similarly, if the "pure experience" of the room
were a place of intersection of two processes, which connected it with different groups of associates respectively, it
could be counted twice over, as belonging to either group,
and spoken of loosely as existing in two places, although it
would remain all the time a numerically single thing.

Well, the experience is a member of diverse processes
that can be followed away from it along entirely different
lines. The one self-identical thing has so many relations to
the rest of experience that you can take it in disparate systems of association, and treat it as belonging with opposite
contexts.[8] In one of these contexts it is your "field of consciousness"; in another it is "the room in which you sit," and
it enters both contexts in its wholeness, giving no pretext
for being said to attach itself to consciousness by one of its
parts or aspects, and to outer reality by another. What are
the two processes, now, into which the room-experience
simultaneously enters in this way?

One of them is the reader's personal biography, the other
is the history of the house of which the room is part. The
presentation, the experience, the *that* in short (for until we
have decided *what* it is it must be a mere *that*) is the last
term of a train of sensations, emotions, decisions, movements, classifications, expectations, etc., ending in the present, and the first term of a series of "inner" operations
extending into the future, on the reader's part. On the other
hand, the very same *that* is the *terminus ad quem* of a lot of
previous physical operations, carpentering, papering, fur-
nishing, warming, etc., and the *terminus a quo* of a lot of
future ones, in which it will be concerned when undergoing
the destiny of a physical room. The physical and the mental
operations form curiously incompatible groups. As a room,
the experience has occupied that spot and had that environment for thirty years. As your field of consciousness it
may never have existed until now. As a room, attention will

---

[8] [Cf. below, "The Essence of Humanism," §II. ED.]

go on to discover endless new details in it. As your mental state merely, few new ones will emerge under attention's eye. As a room, it will take an earthquake, or a gang of men, and in any case a certain amount of time, to destroy it. As your subjective state, the closing of your eyes, or any instantaneous play of your fancy will suffice. In the real world, fire will consume it. In your mind, you can let fire play over it without effect. As an outer object, you must pay so much a month to inhabit it. As an inner content, you may occupy it for any length of time rent-free. If, in short, you follow it in the mental direction, taking it along with events of personal biography solely, all sorts of things are true of it which are false, and false of it which are true if you treat it as a real thing experienced, follow it in the physical direction, and relate it to associates in the outer world.

III

So far, all seems plain sailing, but my thesis will probably grow less plausible to the reader when I pass from percepts to concepts, or from the case of things presented to that of things remote. I believe, nevertheless, that here also the same law holds good. If we take conceptual manifolds, or memories, or fancies, they also are in their first intention mere bits of pure experience, and, as such, are single *thats* which act in one context as objects, and in another context figure as mental states. By taking them in their first intention, I mean ignoring their relation to possible perceptual experiences with which they may be connected, which they may lead to and terminate in, and which then they may be supposed to "represent." Taking them in this way first, we confine the problem to a world merely "thought-of" and not directly felt or seen.[9] This world, just like the world of per-

---

[9] [For the author's recognition of "concepts as a co-ordinate realm" of reality, cf. his *Meaning of Truth,* pp. 42, 195, note; *A Pluralistic Universe,* pp. 339–340; *Some Problems of Philosophy,* pp. 50–57, 67–70; and below, p. 9, note 10. Giving this view the name "logical realism," he remarks elsewhere that his philosophy "may be regarded as somewhat eccentric in its attempt to combine logical realism with an otherwise empiricist mode of thought" (*Some Problems of Philosophy,* p. 106). ED.]

cepts, comes to us at first as a chaos of experiences, but lines of order soon get traced. We find that any bit of it which we may cut out as an example is connected with distinct groups of associates, just as our perceptual experiences are, that these associates link themselves with it by different relations,[10] and that one forms the inner history of a person, while the other acts as an impersonal "objective" world, either spatial and temporal, or else merely logical or mathematical, or otherwise "ideal."

The first obstacle on the part of the reader to seeing that these non-perceptual experiences have objectivity as well as subjectivity will probably be due to the intrusion into his mind of *percepts,* that third group of associates with which the non-perceptual experiences have relations, and which, as a whole, they "represent," standing to them as thoughts to things. This important function of the non-perceptual experiences complicates the question and confuses it; for, so used are we to treat percepts as the sole genuine realities that, unless we keep them out of the discussion, we tend altogether to overlook the objectivity that lies in non-perceptual experiences by themselves. We treat them, "knowing" percepts as they do, as through and through subjective, and say that they are wholly constituted of the stuff called consciousness, using this term now for a kind of entity, after the fashion which I am seeking to refute.[11]

Abstracting, then, from percepts altogether, what I maintain is, that any single non-perceptual experience tends to get counted twice over, just as a perceptual experience does, figuring in one context as an object or field of objects, in another as a state of mind: and all this without the least internal self-diremption on its own part into consciousness

---

[10] Here as elsewhere the relations are of course *experienced* relations, members of the same originally chaotic manifold of non-perceptual experience of which the related terms themselves are parts. [Cf. below, pp. 22–23.]

[11] Of the representative function of non-perceptual experience as a whole, I will say a word in a subsequent article: it leads too far into the general theory of knowledge for much to be said about it in a short paper like this. [Cf. below, "A World of Pure Experience," §III.]

and content. It is all consciousness in one taking; and, in the other, all content.

I find this objectivity of non-perceptual experiences, this complete parallelism in point of reality between the presently felt and the remotely thought, so well set forth in a page of Münsterberg's *Grundzüge,* that I will quote it as it stands.

"I may only think of my objects," says Professor Münsterberg; "yet, in my living thought they stand before me exactly as perceived objects would do, no matter how different the two ways of apprehending them may be in their genesis. The book here lying on the table before me, and the book in the next room of which I think and which I mean to get, are both in the same sense given realities for me, realities which I acknowledge and of which I take account. If you agree that the perceptual object is not an idea within me, but that percept and thing, as indistinguishably one, are really experienced *there, outside,* you ought not to believe that the merely thought-of object is hid away inside of the thinking subject. The object of which I think, and of whose existence I take cognizance without letting it now work upon my senses, occupies its definite place in the outer world as much as does the object which I directly see."

"What is true of the here and the there, is also true of the now and the then. I know of the thing which is present and perceived, but I know also of the thing which yesterday was but is no more, and which I only remember. Both can determine my present conduct, both are parts of the reality of which I keep account. It is true that of much of the past I am uncertain, just as I am uncertain of much of what is present if it be but dimly perceived. But the interval of time does not in principle alter my relation to the object, does not transform it from an object known into a mental state. . . . The things in the room here which I survey, and those in my distant home of which I think, the things of this minute and those of my long-vanished boyhood, influence and decide me alike, with a reality which my experience of them directly feels. They both make up my real world, they make it directly, they do not have first to be introduced to me and mediated by ideas which now and here arise within me. . . . This not-me character of my recollections and expectations does not imply that the external objects of which I am aware in those experiences should necessarily be there also for others. The objects of dreamers and hallucinated persons are wholly without general validity. But even were they centaurs and golden mountains, they still would be 'off there,' in fairy land, and not 'inside' of ourselves."[12]

This certainly is the immediate, primary, naïf, or practical way of taking our thought-of world. Were there no perceptual world to serve as its "reductive," in Taine's sense, by being "stronger" and more genuinely "outer" (so that the whole merely thought-of world seems weak and inner in comparison), our world of thought would be the only world, and would enjoy complete reality in our belief. This actually happens in our dreams, and in our day-dreams so long as percepts do not interrupt them.

And yet, just as the seen room (to go back to our late example) is *also* a field of consciousness, so the conceived or recollected room is *also* a state of mind; and the doubling-up of the experience has in both cases similar grounds.

The room thought-of, namely, has many thought-of couplings with many thought-of things. Some of these couplings are inconstant, others are stable. In the reader's personal history the room occupies a single date—he saw it only once perhaps, a year ago. Of the house's history, on the other hand, it forms a permanent ingredient. Some couplings have the curious stubbornness, to borrow Royce's term, of fact; others show the fluidity of fancy—we let them come and go as we please. Grouped with the rest of its house, with the name of its town, of its owner, builder, value, decorative plan, the room maintains a definite foothold, to which, if we try to loosen it, it tends to return, and to reassert itself with force.[13] With these associates, in

---

[12] Münsterberg: *Grundzüge der Psychologie,* vol. I, p. 48.
[13] Cf. A. L. Hodder: *The Adversaries of the Sceptic,* pp. 94–99.

a word, it coheres, while to other houses, other towns, other owners, etc., it shows no tendency to cohere at all. The two collections, first of its cohesive, and, second, of its loose associates, inevitably come to be contrasted. We call the first collection the system of external realities, in the midst of which the room, as "real," exists; the other we call the stream of our internal thinking, in which, as a "mental image," it for a moment floats.[14] The room thus again gets counted twice over. It plays two different rôles, being *Gedanke* and *Gedachtes,* the thought-of-an-object, and the object-thought-of, both in one; and all this without paradox or mystery, just as the same material thing may be both low and high, or small and great, or bad and good, because of its relations to opposite parts of an environing world.

As "subjective" we say that the experience represents; as "objective" it is represented. What represents and what is represented is here numerically the same; but we must remember that no dualism of being represented and representing resides in the experience *per se.* In its pure state, or when isolated, there is no self-splitting of it into consciousness and what the consciousness is "of." Its subjectivity and objectivity are functional attributes solely, realized only when the experience is "taken," *i.e.,* talked-of, twice, considered along with its two differing contexts respectively, by a new retrospective experience, of which that whole past complication now forms the fresh content.

The instant field of the present is at all times what I call the "pure" experience. It is only virtually or potentially either object or subject as yet. For the time being, it is plain, unqualified actuality, or existence, a simple *that.* In this *naïf* immediacy it is of course *valid*; it is *there,* we *act* upon it; and the doubling of it in retrospection into a state of mind and a reality intended thereby, is just one of the acts.

---

[14] For simplicity's sake I confine my exposition to "external" reality. But there is also the system of ideal reality in which the room plays its part. Relations of comparison, of classification, serial order, value, also are stubborn, assign a definite place to the room, unlike the incoherence of its places in the mere rhapsody of our successive thoughts.

The "state of mind," first treated explicitly as such in retrospection, will stand corrected or confirmed, and the retrospective experience in its turn will get a similar treatment; but the immediate experience in its passing is always "truth,"[15] practical truth, *something to act on,* at its own movement. If the world were then and there to go out like a candle, it would remain truth absolute and objective, for it would be "the last word," would have no critic, and no one would ever oppose the thought in it to the reality intended.[16]

I think I may now claim to have made my thesis clear. Consciousness connotes a kind of external relation, and does not denote a special stuff or way of being. *The peculiarity of our experiences, that they not only are, but are known, which their "conscious" quality is invoked to explain, is better explained by their relations—these relations themselves being experiences—to one another.*

IV

Were I now to go on to treat of the knowing of perceptual by conceptual experiences, it would again prove to be an affair of external relations. One experience would be the knower, the other the reality known; and I could perfectly well define, without the notion of "consciousness," what the knowing actually and practically amounts to—leading-towards, namely, and terminating-in percepts, through a series of transitional experiences which the world supplies.

---

[15] Note the ambiguity of this term, which is taken sometimes objectively and sometimes subjectively.

[16] In the *Psychological Review* for July [1904], Dr. R. B. Perry has published a view of Consciousness which comes nearer to mine than any other with which I am acquainted. At present, Dr. Perry thinks, every field of experience is so much "fact." It becomes "opinion" or "thought" only in retrospection, when a fresh experience, thinking the same object, alters and corrects it. But the corrective experience becomes itself in turn corrected, and thus the experience as a whole is a process in which what is objective originally forever turns subjective, turns into our apprehension of the object. I strongly recommend Dr. Perry's admirable article to my readers.

But I will not treat of this, space being insufficient.[17] I will rather consider a few objections that are sure to be urged against the entire theory as it stands.

V

First of all, this will be asked: "If experience has not 'conscious' existence, if it be not partly made of 'consciousness,' of what then is it made? Matter we know, and thought we know, and conscious content we know, but neutral and simple 'pure experience' is something we know not at all. Say *what* it consists of—for it must consist of something—or be willing to give it up!"

To this challenge the reply is easy. Although for fluency's sake I myself spoke early in this article of a stuff of pure experience, I have now to say that there is no *general* stuff of which experience at large is made. There are as many stuffs as there are "natures" in the things experienced. If you ask what any one bit of pure experience is made of, the answer is always the same: "It is made of *that,* of just what appears, of space, of intensity, of flatness, brownness, heaviness, or what not." Shadworth Hodgson's analysis here leaves nothing to be desired.[18] Experience is only a collective name for all these sensible natures, and save for time and space (and, if you like, for "being") there appears no universal element of which all things are made.

VI

The next objection is more formidable, in fact it sounds quite crushing when one hears it first.

"If it be the self-same piece of pure experience, taken

---

[17] I have given a partial account of the matter in *Mind,* vol. X, p. 27, 1885 [reprinted in *The Meaning of Truth,* pp. 1–42], and in the *Psychological Review,* vol. II, p. 105, 1895 [partly reprinted in *The Meaning of Truth,* pp. 43–50]. See also C. A. Strong's article in the *Journal of Philosophy, Psychology and Scientific Methods,* vol. I, p. 253, May 12, 1904. I hope myself very soon to recur to the matter. [See below, "A World of Pure Experience," §III.]

[18] [Cf. Shadworth Hodgson: *The Metaphysic of Experience,* vol. I, *passim; The Philosophy of Reflection,* bk. II, ch. IV, §3. ED.]

twice over, that serves now as thought and now as thing"—
so the objection runs—"how comes it that its attributes
should differ so fundamentally in the two takings. As thing,
the experience is extended; as thought, it occupies no space
or place. As thing, it is red, hard, heavy; but who ever heard
of a red, hard or heavy thought? Yet even now you said that
an experience is made of just what appears, and what
appears is just such adjectives. How can the one experience
in its thing-function be made of them, consist of them, carry
them as its own attributes, while in its thought-function it
disowns them and attributes them elsewhere. There is a
self-contradiction here from which the radical dualism of
thought and thing is the only truth that can save us. Only
if the thought is one kind of being can the adjectives exist
in it 'intentionally' (to use the scholastic term); only if the
thing is another kind, can they exist in it constitutively and
energetically. No simple subject can take the same adjectives and at one time be qualified by it, and at another time
be merely 'of' it, as of something only meant or known."

The solution insisted on by this objector, like many other
common-sense solutions, grows the less satisfactory the
more one turns it in one's mind. To begin with, *are* thought
and thing as heterogeneous as is commonly said?

No one denies that they have some categories in common.
Their relations to time are identical. Both, moreover, may
have parts (for psychologists in general treat thoughts as
having them); and both may be complex or simple. Both are
of kinds, can be compared, added and subtracted and
arranged in serial orders. All sorts of adjectives qualify our
thoughts which appear incompatible with consciousness,
being as such a bare diaphaneity. For instance, they are
natural and easy, or laborious. They are beautiful, happy,
intense, interesting, wise, idiotic, focal, marginal, insipid,
confused, vague, precise, rational, causal, general, particular, and many things besides. Moreover, the chapters on
"Perception" in the psychology-books are full of facts that
make for the essential homogeneity of thought with thing.
How, if "subject" and "object" were separated "by the whole

diameter of being," and had no attributes in common, could it be so hard to tell, in a presented and recognized material object, what part comes in through the sense-organs and what part comes "out of one's own head"? Sensations and apperceptive ideas fuse here so intimately that you can no more tell where one begins and the other ends, than you can tell, in those cunning circular panoramas that have lately been exhibited, where the real foreground and the painted canvas join together.[19]

Descartes for the first time defined thought as the absolutely unextended, and later philosophers have accepted the description as correct. But what possible meaning has it to say that, when we think of a foot-rule or a square yard, extension is not attributable to our thought? Of every extended object the *adequate* mental picture must have all the extension of the object itself. The difference between objective and subjective extension is one of relation to a context solely. In the mind the various extents maintain no necessarily stubborn order relatively to each other, while in the physical world they bound each other stably, and, added together, make the great enveloping Unit which we believe in and call real Space. As "outer," they carry themselves adversely, so to speak, to one another, exclude one another and maintain their distances; while, as "inner," their order is loose, and they form a *durcheinander* in which unity is lost.[20] But to argue from this that inner experience is absolutely inextensive seems to me little short of absurd. The two worlds differ, not by the presence or absence of extension, but by the relations of the extensions which in both worlds exist.

---

[19] Spencer's proof of his "Transfigured Realism" (his doctrine that there is an absolutely non-mental reality) comes to mind as a splendid instance of the impossibility of establishing radical heterogeneity between thought and thing. All his painfully accumulated points of difference run gradually into their opposites, and are full of exceptions. [Cf. Spencer: *Principles of Psychology,* part VII, ch. XIX.]

[20] I speak here of the complete inner life in which the mind plays freely with its materials. Of course the mind's free play is restricted when it seeks to copy real things in real space.

Does not this case of extension now put us on the track of truth in the case of other qualities? It does; and I am surprised that the facts should not have been noticed long ago. Why, for example, do we call a fire hot, and water wet, and yet refuse to say that our mental state, when it is "of" these objects, is either wet or hot? "Intentionally," at any rate, and when the mental state is a vivid image, hotness and wetness are in it just as much as they are in the physical experience. The reason is this, that, as the general chaos of all our experiences gets sifted, we find that there are some fires that will always burn sticks and always warm our bodies, and that there are some waters that will always put out fires; while there are other fires and waters that will not act at all. The general group of experiences that *act,* that do not only possess their natures intrinsically, but wear them adjectively and energetically, turning them against one another, comes inevitably to be contrasted with the group whose members, having identically the same natures, fail to manifest them in the "energetic" way.[21] I make for myself now an experience of blazing fire; I place it near my body; but it does not warm me in the least. I lay a stick upon it, and the stick either burns or remains green, as I please. I call up water, and pour it on the fire, and absolutely no difference ensues. I account for all such facts by calling this whole train of experiences unreal, a mental train. Mental fire is what won't burn real sticks; mental water is what won't necessarily (though of course it may) put out even a mental fire. Mental knives may be sharp, but they won't cut real wood. Mental triangles are pointed, but their points won't wound. With "real" objects, on the contrary, consequences always accrue; and thus the real experiences get sifted from the mental ones, the things from our thoughts of them, fanciful or true, and precipitated together as the stable part of the whole experience-chaos, under the name of the physical world. Of this our perceptual experiences are

---

[21] [But there are also "mental activity trains," in which thoughts do "work on each other." Cf. essay VI below, "The Experience of Activity," note 16. ED.]

the nucleus, they being the originally *strong* experiences. We add a lot of conceptual experiences to them, making these strong also in imagination, and building out the remoter parts of the physical world by their means; and around this core of reality the world of laxly connected fancies and mere rhapsodical objects floats like a bank of clouds. In the clouds, all sorts of rules are violated which in the core are kept. Extensions there can be indefinitely located; motion there obeys no Newton's laws.

VII

There is a peculiar class of experiences to which, whether we take them as subjective or as objective, we *assign* their several natures as attributes, because in both contexts they affect their associates actively, though in neither quite as "strongly" or as sharply as things affect one another by their physical energies. I refer here to *appreciations,* which form an ambiguous sphere of being, belonging with emotion on the one hand, and having objective "value" on the other, yet seeming not quite inner nor quite outer, as if a diremption had begun but had not made itself complete.[22]

Experiences of painful objects, for example, are usually also painful experiences; perceptions of loveliness, of ugliness, tend to pass muster as lovely or as ugly perceptions; intuitions of the morally lofty are lofty intuitions. Sometimes the adjective wanders as if uncertain where to fix itself. Shall we speak of seductive visions or of visions of seductive things? Of wicked desires or of desires for wickedness? Of healthy thoughts or of thoughts of healthy objects? Of good impulses, or of impulses towards the good? Of feelings of anger, or of angry feelings? Both in the mind and in the thing, these natures modify their context, exclude certain associates and determine others, have their mates and incompatibles. Yet not as stubbornly as in the case of physical qualities, for beauty and ugliness, love and hatred,

---

[22] [This topic is resumed below in essay V, "The Place of Affectional Facts. . . ." ED.]

pleasant and painful can, in certain complex experiences, coexist.

If one were to make an evolutionary construction of how a lot of originally chaotic pure experiences became gradually differentiated into an orderly inner and outer world, the whole theory would turn upon one's success in explaining how or why the quality of an experience, once active, could become less so, and, from being an energetic attribute in some cases, elsewhere lapse into the status of an inert or merely internal "nature." This would be the "evolution" of the psychical from the bosom of the physical, in which the esthetic, moral and otherwise emotional experiences would represent a halfway stage.

VIII

But a last cry of *non possumus* will probably go up from many readers. "All very pretty as a piece of ingenuity," they will say, "but our consciousness itself intuitively contradicts you. We, for our part, *know* that we are conscious. We *feel* our thought, flowing as a life within us, in absolute contrast with the objects which it so unremittingly escorts. We can not be faithless to this immediate intuition. The dualism is a fundamental *datum:* Let no man join what God has put asunder."

My reply to this is my last word, and I greatly grieve that to many it will sound materialistic. I can not help that, however, for I, too, have my intuitions and I must obey them. Let the case be what it may in others, I am as confident as I am of anything that, in myself, the stream of thinking (which I recognize emphatically as a phenomenon) is only a careless name for what, when scrutinized, reveals itself to consist chiefly of the stream of my breathing. The "I think" which Kant said must be able to accompany all my objects, is the "I breathe" which actually does accompany them. There are other internal facts besides breathing (intracephalic muscular adjustments, etc., of which I have said a word in my larger Psychology), and these increase the assets of "consciousness," so far as the latter is subject to immediate perception;[23] but breath, which was ever the original of "spirit," breath moving outwards, between the glottis and the nostrils, is, I am persuaded, the essence out of which philosophers have constructed the entity known to them as consciousness. *That entity is fictitious, while thoughts in the concrete are fully real. But thoughts in the concrete are made of the same stuff as things are.*

I wish I might believe myself to have made that plausible in this article. In another article I shall try to make the general notion of a world composed of pure experiences still more clear.

---

[23] [*Principles of Psychology,* vol. I, pp. 299–305. Cf. essay VI below, "The Experience of Activity," note 13.]

II

A WORLD OF PURE EXPERIENCE[1]

It is difficult not to notice a curious unrest in the philosophic atmosphere of the time, a loosening of old landmarks, a softening of oppositions, a mutual borrowing from one another on the part of systems anciently closed, and an interest in new suggestions, however vague, as if the one thing sure were the inadequacy of the extant school-solutions. The dissatisfaction with these seems due for the most part to a feeling that they are too abstract and academic. Life is confused and superabundant, and what the younger generation appears to crave is more of the temperament of life in its philosophy, even though it were at some cost of logical rigor and of formal purity. Transcendental idealism is inclining to let the world wag incomprehensibly, in spite of its Absolute Subject and his unity of purpose. Berkeleyan idealism is abandoning the principle of parsimony and dabbling in panpsychic speculations. Empiricism flirts with teleology; and, strangest of all, natural realism, so long decently buried, raises its head above the turf, and finds glad hands outstretched from the most unlikely quarters to help it to its feet again. We are all biased by our personal feelings, I know, and I am personally discontented with extant solutions; so I seem to read the signs of a great unsettlement, as if the upheaval of more real conceptions and more fruitful methods were imminent, as if a true land-

---

[1] [Reprinted from the *Journal of Philosophy, Psychology and Scientific Methods,* vol. I, 1904, No. 20, September 29, and No. 21, October 13. Sections III–V have also been reprinted, with some omissions, alterations, and additions, in *The Meaning of Truth,* pp. 102–120. The alterations have been adopted in the present text. ED.]

scape might result, less clipped, straight-edged and artificial.

If philosophy be really on the eve of any considerable rearrangement, the time should be propitious for any one who has suggestions of his own to bring forward. For many years past my mind has been growing into a certain type of *Weltanschauung*. Rightly or wrongly, I have got to the point where I can hardly see things in any other pattern. I propose, therefore, to describe the pattern as clearly as I can consistently with great brevity, and to throw my description into the bubbling vat of publicity where, jostled by rivals and torn by critics, it will eventually either disappear from notice, or else, if better luck befall it, quietly subside to the profundities, and serve as a possible ferment of new growths or a nucleus of new crystallization.

I. RADICAL EMPIRICISM

I give the name of "radical empiricism" to my *Weltanschauung*. Empiricism is known as the opposite of rationalism. Rationalism tends to emphasize universals and to make wholes prior to parts in the order of logic as well as in that of being. Empiricism, on the contrary, lays the explanatory stress upon the part, the element, the individual, and treats the whole as a collection and the universal as an abstraction. My description of things, accordingly, starts with the parts and makes of the whole a being of the second order. It is essentially a mosaic philosophy, a philosophy of plural facts, like that of Hume and his descendants, who refer these facts neither to Substances in which they inhere nor to an Absolute Mind that creates them as its objects. But it differs from the Humian type of empiricism in one particular which makes me add the epithet radical.

To be radical, an empiricism must neither admit into its constructions any element that is not directly experienced, nor exclude from them any element that is directly experienced. For such a philosophy, *the relations that connect experiences must themselves be experienced relations, and any kind of relation experienced must be accounted as "real" as anything else in the system.* Elements may indeed be redistributed, the original placing of things getting corrected, but a real place must be found for every kind of thing experienced, whether term or relation, in the final philosophic arrangement.

Now, ordinary empiricism, in spite of the fact that conjunctive and disjunctive relations present themselves as being fully co-ordinate parts of experience, has always shown a tendency to do away with the connections of things, and to insist most on the disjunctions. Berkeley's nominalism, Hume's statement that whatever things we distinguish are as "loose and separate" as if they had "no manner of connection," James Mill's denial that similars have anything "really" in common, the resolution of the causal tie into habitual sequence, John Mill's account of both physical things and selves as composed of discontinuous possibilities, and the general pulverization of all Experience by association and the mind-dust theory, are examples of what I mean.[2]

The natural result of such a world-picture has been the efforts of rationalism to correct its incoherencies by the addition of trans-experiential agents of unification, substances, intellectual categories and powers, or Selves; whereas, if empiricism had only been radical and taken everything that comes without disfavor, conjunction as well as separation, each at its face value, the results would have called for no such artificial correction. *Radical empiricism, as I understand it, does full justice to conjunctive relations,* without, however, treating them as rationalism always tends to treat them, as being true in some supernal way, as if the unity of things and their variety belonged to different orders of truth and vitality altogether.

---

[2] [Cf. Berkeley: *Principles of Human Knowledge,* Introduction; Hume: *An Enquiry Concerning Human Understanding,* sect. VII, part II (Selby-Bigge's edition, p. 74); James Mill: *Analysis of the Phenomena of the Human Mind,* ch. VIII; J. S. Mill: *An Examination of Sir William Hamilton's Philosophy,* ch. XI, XII; W. K. Clifford: *Lectures and Essays,* pp. 274 ff.]

II. Conjunctive Relations

Relations are of different degrees of intimacy. Merely to be "with" one another in a universe of discourse is the most external relation that terms can have, and seems to involve nothing whatever as to farther consequences. Simultaneity and time-interval come next, and then space-adjacency and distance. After them, similarity and difference, carrying the possibility of many inferences. Then relations of activity, tying terms into series involving change, tendency, resistance, and the causal order generally. Finally, the relation experienced between terms that form states of mind, and are immediately conscious of continuing each other. The organization of the Self as a system of memories, purposes, strivings, fulfilments or disappointments, is incidental to this most intimate of all relations, the terms of which seem in many cases actually to compenetrate and suffuse each other's being.[3]

Philosophy has always turned on grammatical particles. With, near, next, like, from, towards, against, because, for, through, my—these words designate types of conjunctive relation arranged in a roughly ascending order of intimacy and inclusiveness. *A priori,* we can imagine a universe of withness but no nextness; or one of nextness but no likeness, or of likeness with no activity, or of activity with no purpose, or of purpose with no ego. These would be universes, each with its own grade of unity. The universe of human experience is, by one or another of its parts, of each and all these grades. Whether or not it possibly enjoys some still more absolute grade of union does not appear upon the surface.

Taken as it does appear, our universe is to a large extent chaotic. No one single type of connection runs through all the experiences that compose it. If we take space-relations, they fail to connect minds into any regular system. Causes and purposes obtain only among special series of facts. The self-relation seems extremely limited and does not link two different selves together. *Prima facie,* if you should liken

---

[3] [See essay VI below, "The Experience of Activity."]

the universe of absolute idealism to an aquarium, a crystal globe in which goldfish are swimming, you would have to compare the empiricist universe to something more like one of those dried human heads with which the Dyaks of Borneo deck their lodges. The skull forms a solid nucleus; but innumerable feathers, leaves, strings, beads, and loose appendices of every description float and dangle from it, and, save that they terminate in it, seem to have nothing to do with one another. Even so my experiences and yours float and dangle, terminating, it is true, in a nucleus of common perception, but for the most part out of sight and irrelevant and unimaginable to one another. This imperfect intimacy, this bare relation of *withness* between some parts of the sum total of experience and other parts, is the fact that ordinary empiricism over-emphasizes against rationalism, the latter always tending to ignore it unduly. Radical empiricism, on the contrary, is fair to both the unity and the disconnection. It finds no reason for treating either as illusory. It allots to each its definite sphere of description, and agrees that there appear to be actual forces at work which tend, as time goes on, to make the unity greater.

The conjunctive relation that has given most trouble to philosophy is *the co-conscious transition,* so to call it, by which one experience passes into another when both belong to the same self. About the facts there is no question. My experiences and your experiences are "with" each other in various external ways, but mine pass into mine, and yours pass into yours in a way in which yours and mine never pass into one another. Within each of our personal histories, subject, object, interest and purpose *are continuous or may be continuous.*[4] Personal histories are processes of change in time, and *the change itself is one of the things immediately experienced.* "Change" in this case means continuous as opposed to discontinuous transition. But continuous

---

[4] The psychology books have of late described the facts here with approximate adequacy. I may refer to the chapters on "The Stream of Thought" and on the Self in my own *Principles of Psychology,* as well as to S. H. Hodgson's *Metaphysic of Experience,* vol. I, ch. VII and VIII.

transition is one sort of a conjunctive relation; and to be a radical empiricist means to hold fast to this conjunctive relation of all others, for this is the strategic point, the position through which, if a hole be made, all the corruptions of dialectics and all the metaphysical fictions pour into our philosophy. The holding fast to this relation means taking it at its face value, neither less nor more; and to take it at its face value means first of all to take it just as we feel it, and not to confuse ourselves with abstract talk *about* it, involving words that drive us to invent secondary conceptions in order to neutralize their suggestions and to make our actual experience again seem rationally possible.

What I do feel simply when a later moment of my experience succeeds an earlier one is that though they are two moments, the transition from the one to the other is *continuous*. Continuity here is a definite sort of experience; just as definite as is the *discontinuity-experience* which I find it impossible to avoid when I seek to make the transition from an experience of my own to one of yours. In this latter case I have to get on and off again, to pass from a thing lived to another thing only conceived, and the break is positively experienced and noted. Though the functions exerted by my experience and by yours may be the same (*e.g.,* the same objects known and the same purposes followed), yet the sameness has in this case to be ascertained expressly (and often with difficulty and uncertainty) after the break has been felt; whereas in passing from one of my own moments to another the sameness of object and interest is unbroken, and both the earlier and the later experience are of things directly lived.

There is no other *nature,* no other whatness than this absence of break and this sense of continuity in that most intimate of all conjunctive relations, the passing of one experience into another when they belong to the same self. And this whatness is real empirical "content," just as the whatness of separation and discontinuity is real content in the contrasted case. Practically to experience one's personal continuum in this living way is to know the originals of the ideas of continuity and sameness, to know what the words stand for concretely, to own all that they can ever mean. But all experiences have their conditions; and over-subtle intellects, thinking about the facts here, and asking how they are possible, have ended by substituting a lot of static objects of conception for the direct perceptual experiences. "Sameness," they have said, "must be a stark numerical identity; it can't run on from next to next. Continuity can't mean mere absence of gap; for if you say two things are in immediate contact, *at* the contact how can they be two? If, on the other hand, you put a relation of transition between them, that itself is a third thing, and needs to be related or hitched to its terms. An infinite series is involved," and so on. The result is that from difficulty to difficulty, the plain conjunctive experience has been discredited by both schools, the empiricists leaving things permanently disjoined, and the rationalists remedying the looseness by their Absolutes or Substances, or whatever other fictitious agencies of union they may have employed.[5] From all which artificiality we can be saved by a couple of simple reflections: first, that conjunctions and separations are, at all events, co-ordinate phenomena which, if we take experiences at their face value, must be accounted equally real; and second, that if we insist on treating things as really separate when they are given as continuously joined, invoking, when union is required, transcendental principles to overcome the separateness we have assumed, then we ought to stand ready to perform the converse act. We ought to invoke higher principles of *dis*union, also, to make our merely experienced *dis*junctions more truly real. Failing thus, we ought to let the originally given continuities stand on their own bottom. We have no right to be lopsided or to blow capriciously hot and cold.

III. THE COGNITIVE RELATION

The first great pitfall from which such a radical standing by experience will save us is an artificial conception of the

---

[5] [See the following essay, "The Thing and Its Relations."]

relations between knower and known. Throughout the history of philosophy the subject and its object have been treated as absolutely discontinuous entities; and thereupon the presence of the latter to the former, or the "apprehension" by the former of the latter, has assumed a paradoxical character which all sorts of theories had to be invented to overcome. Representative theories put a mental "representation," "image," or "content" into the gap, as a sort of intermediary. Common-sense theories left the gap untouched, declaring our mind able to clear it by a self-transcending leap. Transcendentalist theories left it impossible to traverse by finite knowers, and brought an Absolute in to perform the saltatory act. All the while, in the very bosom of the finite experience, every conjunction required to make the relation intelligible is given in full. Either the knower and the known are:

(1) the self-same piece of experience taken twice over in different contexts; or they are

(2) two pieces of *actual* experience belonging to the same subject, with definite tracts of conjunctive transitional experience between them; or

(3) the known is a *possible* experience either of that subject or another, to which the said conjunctive transitions *would* lead, if sufficiently prolonged.

To discuss all the ways in which one experience may function as the knower of another, would be incompatible with the limits of this essay.[6] I have just treated of type 1, the kind of knowledge called perception.[7] This is the type of case in which the mind enjoys direct "acquaintance" with a present object. In the other types the mind has "knowledge-about" an object not immediately there. Of type 2, the sim-

---

[6] For brevity's sake I altogether omit mention of the type constituted by knowledge of the truth of general propositions. This type has been thoroughly and, so far as I can see, satisfactorily, elucidated in Dewey's *Studies in Logical Theory.* Such propositions are reducible to the *S*-is-*P* form; and the "terminus" that verifies and fulfils is the *SP* in combination. Of course percepts may be involved in the mediating experiences, or in the "satisfactoriness" of the *P* in its new position.

[7] [See essay I above, "Does 'Consciousness' Exist?" §II.]

plest sort of conceptual knowledge, I have given some account in two articles.[8] Type 3 can always formally and hypothetically be reduced to type 2, so that a brief description of that type will put the present reader sufficiently at my point of view, and make him see what the actual meanings of the mysterious cognitive relation may be.

Suppose me to be sitting here in my library at Cambridge, at ten minutes' walk from "Memorial Hall," and to be thinking truly of the latter object. My mind may have before it only the name, or it may have a clear image, or it may have a very dim image of the hall, but such intrinsic differences in the image make no difference in its cognitive function. Certain *extrinsic* phenomena, special experiences of conjunction, are what impart to the image, be it what it may, its knowing office.

For instance, if you ask me what hall I mean by my image, and I can tell you nothing; or if I fail to point or lead you towards the Harvard Delta; or if, being led by you, I am uncertain whether the Hall I see be what I had in mind or not; you would rightly deny that I had "meant" that particular hall at all, even though my mental image might to some degree have resembled it. The resemblance would count in that case as coincidental merely, for all sorts of things of a kind resemble one another in this world without being held for that reason to take cognizance of one another.

On the other hand, if I can lead you to the hall, and tell you of its history and present uses; if in its presence I feel my idea, however imperfect it may have been, to have led

---

[8]["On the Function of Cognition," *Mind,* vol. X, 1885, and "The Knowing of Things Together," *Psychological Review,* vol. II, 1895. These articles are reprinted, the former in full, the latter in part, in *The Meaning of Truth,* pp. 1–50. ED.] These articles and their doctrine, unnoticed apparently by any one else, have lately gained favorable comment from Professor Strong. ["A Naturalistic Theory of the Reference of Thought to Reality," *Journal of Philosophy, Psychology and Scientific Methods,* vol. I, 1904.] Dr. Dickinson S. Miller has independently thought out the same results ["The Meaning of Truth and Error," *Philosophical Review,* vol. II, 1893; "The Confusion of Function and Content in Mental Analysis," *Psychological Review,* vol. II, 1895], which Strong accordingly dubs the James-Miller theory of cognition.

hither and to be now *terminated;* if the associates of the image and of the felt hall run parallel, so that each term of the one context corresponds serially, as I walk, with an answering term of the others; why then my soul was prophetic, and my idea must be, and by common consent would be, called cognizant of reality. That percept was what I *meant,* for into it my idea has passed by conjunctive experiences of sameness and fulfilled intention. Nowhere is there jar, but every later moment continues and corroborates an earlier one.

In this continuing and corroborating, taken in no transcendental sense, but denoting definitely felt transitions, *lies all that the knowing of a percept by an idea can possibly contain or signify.* Wherever such transitions are felt, the first experience *knows* the last one. Where they do not, or where even as possibles they can not, intervene, there can be no pretense of knowing. In this latter case the extremes will be connected, if connected at all, by inferior relations—bare likeness or succession, or by "withness" alone. Knowledge of sensible realities thus comes to life inside the tissue of experience. It is *made;* and made by relations that unroll themselves in time. Whenever certain intermediaries are given, such that, as they develop towards their terminus, there is experience from point to point of one direction followed, and finally of one process fulfilled, the result is that *their starting-point thereby becomes a knower and their terminus an object meant or known.* That is all that knowing (in the simple case considered) can be known-as, that is the whole of its nature, put into experiential terms. Whenever such is the sequence of our experiences we may freely say that we had the terminal object "in mind" from the outset, even although *at* the outset nothing was there in us but a flat piece of substantive experience like any other, with no self-transcendency about it, and no mystery save the mystery of coming into existence and of being gradually followed by other pieces of substantive experience, with conjunctively transitional experiences between. That is what we *mean* here by the object's being "in mind." Of any deeper more real way of being in mind we have no positive conception, and we have no right to discredit our actual experience by talking of such a way at all.

I know that many a reader will rebel at this. "Mere inter-mediaries," he will say, "even though they be feelings of con-tinuously growing fulfilment, only *separate* the knower from the known, whereas what we have in knowledge is a kind of immediate touch of the one by the other, an 'appre-hension' in the etymological sense of the word, a leaping of the chasm as by lightning, an act by which two terms are smitten into one, over the head of their distinctness. All these dead intermediaries of yours are out of each other, and outside of their termini still."

But do not such dialectic difficulties remind us of the dog dropping his bone and snapping at its image in the water? If we knew any more real kind of union *aliunde,* we might be entitled to brand all our empirical unions as a sham. But unions by continuous transition are the only ones we know of, whether in this matter of a knowledge-about that termi-nates in an acquaintance, whether in personal identity, in logical predication through the copula "is," or elsewhere. If anywhere there were more absolute unions realized, they could only reveal themselves to us by just such conjunctive results. These are what the unions are *worth,* these are all that *we can ever practically mean* by union, by continuity. Is it not time to repeat what Lotze said of substances, that to *act like* one is to *be* one?[9] Should we not say here that to be experienced as continuous is to be really continuous, in a world where experience and reality come to the same thing? In a picture gallery a painted hook will serve to hang a painted chain by, a painted cable will hold a painted ship. In a world where both the terms and their distinctions are affairs of experience, conjunctions that are experienced must be at least as real as anything else. They will be "absolutely" real conjunctions, if we have no transphenom-enal Absolute ready, to derealize the whole experienced world by, at a stroke. If, on the other hand, we had such an

---

[9] [Cf. H. Lotze: *Metaphysik,* §§37–39, 97, 98, 243.]

Absolute, not one of our opponents' theories of knowledge
could remain standing any better than ours could; for the
distinctions as well as the conjunctions of experience would
impartially fall its prey. The whole question of how "one"
thing can know "another" would cease to be a real one at all
in a world where otherness itself was an illusion.[10]

So much for the essentials of the cognitive relation, where
the knowledge is conceptual in type, or forms knowledge
"about" an object. It consists in intermediary experiences
(possible, if not actual) of continuously developing progress,
and, finally, of fulfillment, when the sensible percept, which
is the object, is reached. The percept here not only *verifies*
the concept, proves its function of knowing that percept to
be true, but the percept's existence as the terminus of the
chain of intermediaries *creates* the function. Whatever terminates that chain was, because it now proves itself to be,
what the concept "had in mind."

The towering importance for human life of this kind of
knowing lies in the fact that an experience that knows
another can figure as its *representative,* not in any quasi-
miraculous "epistemological" sense, but in the definite practical sense of being its *substitute* in various operations,
sometimes physical and sometimes mental, which lead us
to its associates and results. By experimenting on our ideas
of reality, we may save ourselves the trouble of experimenting on the real experiences which they severally mean. The
ideas form related systems, corresponding point for point to
the systems which the realities form; and by letting an ideal
term call up its associates systematically, we may be led to
a terminus which the corresponding real term would have
led to in case we had operated on the real world. And this
brings us to the general question of substitution.

---

[10] Mr. Bradley, not professing to know his absolute *aliunde,* nevertheless
derealizes Experience by alleging it to be everywhere infected with self-
contradiction. His arguments seem almost purely verbal, but this is no
place for arguing that point out. [Cf. F. H. Bradley; *Appearance and
Reality, passim;* and essay III below, "The Thing and Its Relations,"
§§IV–V.]

IV. Substitution

In Taine's brilliant book on "Intelligence," substitution was for the first time named as a cardinal logical function, though of course the facts had always been familiar enough. What, exactly, in a system of experiences, does the "substitution" of one of them for another mean?

According to my view, experience as a whole is a process in time, whereby innumerable particular terms lapse and are superseded by others that follow upon them by transitions which, whether disjunctive or conjunctive in content, are themselves experiences, and must in general be accounted at least as real as the terms which they relate. What the nature of the event called "superseding" signifies, depends altogether on the kind of transition that obtains. Some experiences simply abolish their predecessors without continuing them in any way. Others are felt to increase or to enlarge their meaning, to carry out their purpose, or to bring us nearer to their goal. They "represent" them, and may fulfill their function better than they fulfilled it themselves. But to "fulfill a function" in a world of pure experience can be conceived and defined in only one possible way. In such a world transitions and arrivals (or terminations) are the only events that happen, though they happen by so many sorts of path. The only function that one experience can perform is to lead into another experience; and the only fulfillment we can speak of is the reaching of a certain experienced end. When one experience leads to (or can lead to) the same end as another, they agree in function. But the whole system of experiences as they are immediately given presents itself as a quasi-chaos through which one can pass out of an initial term in many directions and yet end in the same terminus, moving from next to next by a great many possible paths.

Either one of these paths might be a functional substitute for another, and to follow one rather than another might on occasion be an advantageous thing to do. As a matter of fact, and in a general way, the paths that run through con-

ceptual experiences, that is, through "thoughts" or "ideas"
that "know" the things in which they terminate, are highly
advantageous paths to follow. Not only do they yield incon-
ceivably rapid transitions; but, owing to the "universal"
character[11] which they frequently possess, and to their
capacity for association with one another in great systems,
they outstrip the tardy consecutions of the things themselves, and sweep us on towards our ultimate termini in a
far more labor-saving way than the following of trains of
sensible perception ever could. Wonderful are the new cuts
and the short-circuits which the thought-paths make. Most
thought-paths, it is true, are substitutes for nothing actual;
they end outside the real world altogether, in wayward fancies, utopias, fictions or mistakes. But where they do re-
enter reality and terminate therein, we substitute them
always; and with these substitutes we pass the greater
number of our hours.

This is why I called our experiences, taken all together, a
quasi-chaos. There is vastly more discontinuity in the sum
total of experiences than we commonly suppose. The objective nucleus of every man's experience, his own body, is, it
is true, a continuous percept; and equally continuous as a
percept (though we may be inattentive to it) is the material
environment of that body, changing by gradual transition
when the body moves. But the distant parts of the physical
world are at all times absent from us, and form conceptual
objects merely, into the perceptual reality of which our life
inserts itself at points discrete and relatively rare. Round
their several objective nuclei, partly shared and common
and partly discrete, of the real physical world, innumerable
thinkers, pursuing their several lines of physically true cog-
itation, trace paths that intersect one another only at discontinuous perceptual points, and the rest of the time are

---

[11] Of which all that need be said in this essay is that it also can be conceived as functional, and defined in terms of transitions, or of the possibility of such. [Cf. *Principles of Psychology,* vol. I, pp. 473–480, vol. II,
pp. 337–340; *Pragmatism,* p. 265; *Some Problems of Philosophy,* pp.
63–74; *Meaning of Truth,* pp. 246–247, etc. ED.]

quite incongruent; and around all the nuclei of shared "reality," as around the Dyak's head of my late metaphor, floats the vast cloud of experiences that are wholly subjective, that are non-substitutional, that find not even an eventual ending for themselves in the perceptual world—the mere day-dreams and joys and sufferings and wishes of the individual minds. These exist *with* one another, indeed, and with the objective nuclei, but out of them it is probable that to all eternity no interrelated system of any kind will ever be made.

This notion of the purely substitutional or conceptual physical world brings us to the most critical of all steps in the development of a philosophy of pure experience. The paradox of self-transcendency in knowledge comes back upon us here, but I think that our notions of pure experience and of substitution, and our radically empirical view of conjunctive transitions, are *Denkmittel* that will carry us safely through the pass.

V. WHAT OBJECTIVE REFERENCE IS

Whosoever feels his experience to be something substitutional even while he has it, may be said to have an experience that reaches beyond itself. From inside of its own entity it says "more," and postulates reality existing elsewhere. For the transcendentalist, who holds knowing to consist in a *salto mortale* across an "epistemological chasm," such an idea presents no difficulty; but it seems at first sight as if it might be inconsistent with an empiricism like our own. Have we not explained that conceptual knowledge is made such wholly by the existence of things that fall outside of the knowing experience itself—by intermediary experiences and by a terminus that fulfills? Can the knowledge be there before these elements that constitute its being have come? And, if knowledge be not there, how can objective reference occur?

The key to this difficulty lies in the distinction between knowing as verified and completed, and the same knowing as in transit and on its way. To recur to the Memorial Hall example lately used, it is only when our idea of the Hall has actually terminated in the percept that we know "for certain" that from the beginning it was truly cognitive of *that*. Until established by the end of the process, its quality of knowing that, or indeed of knowing anything, could still be doubted; and yet the knowing really was there, as the result now shows. We were *virtual* knowers of the Hall long before we were certified to have been its actual knowers, by the percept's retroactive validating power. Just so we are "mortal" all the time, by reason of the virtuality of the inevitable event which will make us so when it shall have come.

Now the immensely greater part of all our knowing never gets beyond this virtual stage. It never is completed or nailed down. I speak not merely of our ideas of imperceptibles like ether-waves or dissociated "ions," or of "ejects" like the contents of our neighbors' minds; I speak also of ideas which we might verify if we would take the trouble, but which we hold for true although unterminated perceptually, because nothing says "no" to us, and there is no contradicting truth in sight. *To continue thinking unchallenged is, ninety-nine times out of a hundred, our practical substitute for knowing in the completed sense.* As each experience runs by cognitive transition into the next one, and we nowhere feel a collision with what we elsewhere count as truth or fact, we commit ourselves to the current as if the port were sure. We live, as it were, upon the front edge of an advancing wave-crest, and our sense of a determinate direction in falling forward is all we cover of the future of our path. It is as if a differential quotient should be conscious and treat itself as an adequate substitute for a traced-out curve. Our experience, *inter alia,* is of variations of rate and of direction, and lives in these transitions more than in the journey's end. The experiences of tendency are sufficient to act upon—what more could we have *done* at those moments even if the later verification comes complete?

This is what, as a radical empiricist, I say to the charge that the objective reference which is so flagrant a character of our experiences involves a chasm and a mortal leap. A positively conjunctive transition involves neither chasm nor leap. Being the very original of what we mean by continuity, it makes a continuum wherever it appears. I know full well that such brief words as these will leave the hardened transcendentalist unshaken. Conjunctive experiences *separate* their terms, he will still say: they are third things interposed, that have themselves to be conjoined by new links, and to invoke them makes our trouble infinitely worse. To "feel" our motion forward is impossible. Motion implies terminus; and how can terminus be felt before we have arrived? The barest start and sally forwards, the barest tendency to leave the instant, involves the chasm and the leap. Conjunctive transitions are the most superficial of appearances, illusions of our sensibility which philosophical reflection pulverizes at a touch. Conception is our only trustworthy instrument, conception and the Absolute working hand in hand. Conception disintegrates experience utterly, but its disjunctions are easily overcome again when the Absolute takes up the task.

Such transcendentalists I must leave, provisionally at least, in full possession of their creed.[12] I have no space for polemics in this article, so I shall simply formulate the empiricist doctrine as my hypothesis, leaving it to work or not work as it may.

Objective reference, I say then, is an incident of the fact that so much of our experience comes as an insufficient and consists of process and transition. Our fields of experience have no more definite boundaries than have our fields of view. Both are fringed forever by a *more* that continuously develops, and that continuously supersedes them as life proceeds. The relations, generally speaking, are as real here as the terms are, and the only complaint of the transcendentalist's with which I could at all sympathize would be his charge that, by first making knowledge consist in external relations as I have done, and by then confessing that nine-tenths of the time these are not actually but only

---

[12] [Cf. essay III below, "The Thing and Its Relations," §I.]

virtually there, I have knocked the solid bottom out of the whole business, and palmed off a substitute of knowledge for the genuine thing. Only the admission, such a critic might say, that our ideas are self-transcendent and "true" already, in advance of the experiences that are to terminate them, can bring solidity back to knowledge in a world like this, in which transitions and terminations are only by exception fulfilled.

This seems to me an excellent place for applying the pragmatic method. When a dispute arises, that method consists in auguring what practical consequences would be different if one side rather than the other were true. If no difference can be thought of, the dispute is a quarrel over words. What then would the self-transcendency affirmed to exist in advance of all experiential mediation or termination, be *known-as?* What would it practically result in for *us,* were it true?

It could only result in our orientation, in the turning of our expectations and practical tendencies into the right path; and the right path here, so long as we and the object are not yet face to face (or can never get face to face, as in the case of ejects), would be the path that led us into the object's nearest neighborhood. Where direct acquaintance is lacking, "knowledge about" is the next best thing, and an acquaintance with what actually lies about the object, and is most closely related to it, puts such knowledge within our grasp. Ether-waves and your anger, for example, are things in which my thoughts will never *perceptually* terminate, but my concepts of them lead me to their very brink, to the chromatic fringes and to the hurtful words and deeds which are their really next effects.

Even if our ideas did in themselves carry the postulated self-transcendency, it would still remain true that their putting us into possession of such effects *would be the sole cash-value of the self-transcendency for us.* And this cash-value, it is needless to say, is *verbatim et literatim* what our empiricist account pays in. On pragmatist principles therefore, a dispute over self-transcendency is a pure logomachy.

Call our concepts of ejective things self-transcendent or the reverse, it makes no difference, so long as we don't differ about the nature of that exalted virtue's fruits—fruits for us, of course, humanistic fruits. If an Absolute were proved to exist for other reasons, it might well appear that *his* knowledge is terminated in innumerable cases where ours is still incomplete. That, however, would be a fact indifferent to our knowledge. The latter would grow neither worse nor better, whether we acknowledged such an Absolute or left him out.

So the notion of a knowledge still *in transitu* and on its way joins hands here with that notion of a "pure experience" which I tried to explain in my [essay] entitled "Does 'Consciousness' Exist?" The instant field of the present is always experience in its "pure" state, plain unqualified actuality, a simple *that,* as yet undifferentiated into thing and thought, and only virtually classifiable as objective fact or as some one's opinion about fact. This is as true when the field is conceptual as when it is perceptual. "Memorial Hall" is "there" in my idea as much as when I stand before it. I proceed to act on its account in either case. Only in the later experience that supersedes the present one is this *naïf* immediacy retrospectively split into two parts, a "consciousness" and its "content," and the content corrected or confirmed. While still pure, or present, any experience—mine, for example, of what I write about in these very lines—passes for "truth." The morrow may reduce it to "opinion." The transcendentalist in all his particular knowledges is as liable to this reduction as I am: his Absolute does not save him. Why, then, need he quarrel with an account of knowing that merely leaves it liable to this inevitable condition? Why insist that knowing is a static relation out of time when it practically seems so much a function of our active life? For a thing to be valid, says Lotze, is the same as to make itself valid. When the whole universe seems only to be making itself valid and to be still incomplete (else why its ceaseless changing?) why, of all things, should knowing be exempt? Why should it not be making itself valid like everything else? That some parts of it may be already valid or verified beyond dispute, the empirical philosopher, of course, like any one else, may always hope.

VI. The Conterminousness of Different Minds[13]

With transition and prospect thus enthroned in pure experience, it is impossible to subscribe to the idealism of the English school. Radical empiricism has, in fact, more affinities with natural realism than with the views of Berkeley or of Mill, and this can be easily shown.

For the Berkeleyan school, ideas (the verbal equivalent of what I term experiences) are discontinuous. The content of each is wholly immanent, and there are no transitions with which they are consubstantial and through which their beings may unite. Your Memorial Hall and mine, even when both are percepts, are wholly out of connection with each other. Our lives are a congeries of solipsisms, out of which in strict logic only a God could compose a universe even of discourse. No dynamic currents run between my objects and your objects. Never can our minds meet in the *same*.

The incredibility of such a philosophy is flagrant. It is "cold, strained, and unnatural" in a supreme degree; and it may be doubted whether even Berkeley himself, who took it so religiously, really believed, when walking through the streets of London, that his spirit and the spirits of his fellow wayfarers had absolutely different towns in view.

To me the decisive reason in favor of our minds meeting in *some* common objects at least is that, unless I make that supposition, I have no motive for assuming that your mind exists at all. Why do I postulate your mind? Because I see your body acting in a certain way. Its gestures, facial movements, words and conduct generally, are "expressive," so I deem it actuated as my own is, by an inner life like mine. This argument from analogy is my *reason*, whether an instinctive belief runs before it or not. But what is "your body" here but a percept in *my* field? It is only as animating

---

[13] [Cf. essay IV below, "How Two Minds Can Know One Thing."]

that object, *my* object, that I have any occasion to think of
you at all. If the body that you actuate be not the very body
that I see there, but some duplicate body of your own with
which that has nothing to do, we belong to different universes, you and I, and for me to speak of you is folly.
Myriads of such universes even now may coexist, irrelevant
to one another; my concern is solely with the universe with
which my own life is connected.

In that perceptual part of *my* universe which I call *your*
body, your mind and my mind meet and may be called conterminous. Your mind actuates that body and mine sees it;
my thoughts pass into it as into their harmonious cognitive
fulfillment; your emotions and volitions pass into it as
causes into their effects.

But that percept hangs together with all our other physical percepts. They are of one stuff with it; and if it be our
common possession, they must be so likewise. For instance,
your hand lays hold of one end of a rope and my hand lays
hold of the other end. We pull against each other. Can our
two hands be mutual objects in this experience, and the
rope not be mutual also? What is true of the rope is true of
any other percept. Your objects are over and over again the
same as mine. If I ask you *where* some object of yours is, our
old Memorial Hall, for example, you point to *my* Memorial
Hall with *your* hand which *I* see. If you alter an object in
your world, put out a candle, for example, when I am present, *my* candle *ipso facto* goes out. It is only as altering my
objects that I guess you to exist. If your objects do not coalesce with my objects, if they be not identically where mine
are, they must be proved to be positively somewhere else.
But no other location can be assigned for them, so their
place must be what it seems to be, the same.[14]

Practically, then, our minds meet in a world of objects
which they share in common, which would still be there, if
one or several of the minds were destroyed. I can see no for-

---

[14] The notion that our objects are inside of our respective heads is not seriously defensible, so I pass it by.

mal objection to this supposition's being literally true. On the principles which I am defending, a "mind" or "personal consciousness" is the name for a series of experiences run together by certain definite transitions, and an objective reality is a series of similar experiences knit by different transitions. If one and the same experience can figure twice, once in a mental and once in a physical context (as I have tried, in my article on "Consciousness," to show that it can), one does not see why it might not figure thrice, or four times, or any number of times, by running into as many different mental contexts, just as the same point, lying at their intersection, can be continued into many different lines. Abolishing any number of contexts would not destroy the experience itself or its other contexts, any more than abolishing some of the point's linear continuations would destroy the others, or destroy the point itself.

I well know the subtle dialectic which insists that a term taken in another relation must needs be an intrinsically different term. The crux is always the old Greek one, that the same man can't be tall in relation to one neighbor, and short in relation to another, for that would make him tall and short at once. In this essay I can not stop to refute this dialectic, so I pass on, leaving my flank for the time exposed.[15] But if my reader will only allow that the same "*now*" both ends his past and begins his future; or that, when he buys an acre of land from his neighbor, it is the same acre that successively figures in the two estates; or that when I pay him a dollar, the same dollar goes into his pocket that came out of mine; he will also in consistency have to allow that the same object may conceivably play a part in, as being related to the rest of, any number of otherwise entirely different minds. This is enough for my present point: the common-sense notion of minds sharing the same object offers no special logical or epistemological difficulties of its own; it stands or falls with the general possi-

---

[15] [The argument is resumed in essay III below, "The Thing and Its Relations," §III. ED.]

bility of things being in conjunctive relation with other things at all.

In principle, then, let natural realism pass for possible. Your mind and mine *may* terminate in the same percept, not merely against it, as if it were a third external thing, but by inserting themselves into it and coalescing with it, for such is the sort of conjunctive union that appears to be experienced when a perceptual terminus "fulfills." Even so, two hawsers may embrace the same pile, and yet neither one of them touch any other part except that pile, of what the other hawser is attached to.

It is therefore not a formal question, but a question of empirical fact solely, whether, when you and I are said to know the "same" Memorial Hall, our minds do terminate at or in a numerically identical percept. Obviously, as a plain matter of fact, they do *not*. Apart from color-blindness and such possibilities, we see the Hall in different perspectives. You may be on one side of it and I on another. The percept of each of us, as he sees the surface of the Hall, is moreover only his provisional terminus. The next thing beyond my percept is not your mind, but more percepts of my own into which my first percept develops, the interior of the Hall, for instance, or the inner structure of its bricks and mortar. If our minds were in a literal sense *con*terminous, neither could get beyond the percept which they had in common, it would be an ultimate barrier between them—unless indeed they flowed over it and became "co-conscious" over a still larger part of their content, which (thought-transference apart) is not supposed to be the case. In point of fact the ultimate common barrier can always be pushed, by both minds, farther than any actual percept of either, until at last it resolves itself into the mere notion of imperceptibles like atoms or ether, so that, where we do terminate in percepts, our knowledge is only speciously completed, being, in theoretic strictness, only a virtual knowledge of those remoter objects which conception carries out.

Is natural realism, permissible in logic, refuted then by empirical fact? Do our minds have no object in common after all?

Yes, they certainly have *Space* in common. On pragmatic principles we are obliged to predicate sameness wherever we can predicate no assignable point of difference. If two named things have every quality and function indiscernible, and are at the same time in the same place, they must be written down as numerically one thing under two different names. But there is no test discoverable, so far as I know, by which it can be shown that the place occupied by your percept of Memorial Hall differs from the place occupied by mine. The percepts themselves may be shown to differ; but if each of us be asked to point out where his percept is, we point to an identical spot. All the relations, whether geometrical or causal, of the Hall originate or terminate in that spot wherein our hands meet, and where each of us begins to work if he wishes to make the Hall change before the other's eyes. Just so it is with our bodies. That body of yours which you actuate and feel from within must be in the same spot as the body of yours which I see or touch from without. "There" for me means where I place my finger. If you do not feel my finger's contact to be "there" in *my* sense, when I place it on your body, where then do you feel it? Your inner actuations of your body meet my finger *there:* it is *there* that you resist its push, or shrink back, or sweep the finger aside with your hand. Whatever farther knowledge either of us may acquire of the real constitution of the body which we thus feel, you from within and I from without, it is in that same place that the newly conceived or perceived constituents have to be located, and it is *through* that space that your and my mental intercourse with each other has always to be carried on, by the mediation of impressions which I convey thither, and of the reactions thence which those impressions may provoke from you.

In general terms, then, whatever differing contents our minds may eventually fill a place with, the place itself is a numerically identical content of the two minds, a piece of common property in which, through which, and over which they join. The receptacle of certain of our experiences being thus common, the experiences themselves might some day become common also. If that day ever did come, our thoughts would terminate in a complete empirical identity, there would be an end, so far as *those* experiences went, to our discussions about truth. No points of difference appearing, they would have to count as the same.

VII. Conclusion

With this we have the outlines of a philosophy of pure experience before us. At the outset of my essay, I called it a mosaic philosophy. In actual mosaics the pieces are held together by their bedding, for which bedding of the Substances, transcendental Egos, or Absolutes of other philosophies may be taken to stand. In radical empiricism there is no bedding; it is as if the pieces clung together by their edges, the transitions experienced between them forming their cement. Of course such a metaphor is misleading, for in actual experience the more substantive and the more transitive parts run into each other continuously, there is in general no separateness needing to be overcome by an external cement; and whatever separateness is actually experienced is not overcome, it stays and counts as separateness to the end. But the metaphor serves to symbolize the fact that Experience itself, taken at large, can grow by its edges. That one moment of it proliferates into the next by transitions which, whether conjunctive or disjunctive, continue the experiential tissue, can not, I contend, be denied. Life is in the transitions as much as in the terms connected; often, indeed, it seems to be there more emphatically, as if our spurts and sallies forward were the real firing-line of the battle, were like the thin line of flame advancing across the dry autumnal field which the farmer proceeds to burn. In this line we live prospectively as well as retrospectively. It is "of" the past, inasmuch as it comes expressly as the past's continuation; it is "of" the future in so far as the future, when it comes, will have continued *it*.

These relations of continuous transition experienced are what make our experiences cognitive. In the simplest and completest cases the experiences are cognitive of one another. When one of them terminates a previous series of them with a sense of fulfillment, it, we say, is what those other experiences "had in view." The knowledge, in such a case, is verified; the truth is "salted down." Mainly, however, we live on speculative investments, or on our prospects only. But living on things *in posse* is as good as living in the actual, so long as our credit remains good. It is evident that for the most part it is good, and that the universe seldom protests our drafts.

In this sense we at every moment can continue to believe in an existing *beyond.* It is only in special cases that our confident rush forward gets rebuked. The beyond must, of course, always in our philosophy be itself of an experiential nature. If not a future experience of our own or a present one of our neighbor, it must be a thing in itself in Dr. Prince's and Professor Strong's sense of the term—that is, it must be an experience *for* itself whose relation to other things we translate into the action of molecules, etherwaves, or whatever else the physical symbols may be.[16] This opens the chapter of the relations of radical empiricism to panpsychism, into which I cannot enter now.[17]

The beyond can in any case exist simultaneously—for it can be experienced *to have existed* simultaneously—with the experience that practically postulates it by looking in its direction, or by turning or changing in the direction of which it is the goal. Pending that actuality of union, in the virtuality of which the "truth," even now, of the postulation consists, the beyond and its knower are entities split off from each other. The world is in so far forth a pluralism of which the unity is not fully experienced as yet. But, as fast as verifications come, trains of experience, once separate,

---

[16] Our minds and these ejective realities would still have space (or pseudo-space, as I believe Professor Strong calls the medium of interaction between "things-in-themselves") in common. These would exist *where,* and begin to act *where,* we locate the molecules, etc., and *where* we perceive the sensible phenomena explained thereby. [Cf. Morton Prince: *The Nature of Mind, and Human Automatism,* part I, ch. III, IV; C. A. Strong: *Why the Mind Has a Body,* ch. XII.]

[17] [Cf. *A Pluralistic Universe,* Lect. IV–VII.]

run into one another; and that is why I said, earlier in my
article, that the unity of the world is on the whole undergoing increase. The universe continually grows in quantity by
new experiences that graft themselves upon the older mass;
but these very new experiences often help the mass to a
more consolidated form.

These are the main features of a philosophy of pure experience. It has innumerable other aspects and arouses innumerable questions, but the points I have touched on seem
enough to make an entering wedge. In my own mind such a
philosophy harmonizes best with a radical pluralism, with
novelty and indeterminism, moralism and theism, and with
the "humanism" lately sprung upon us by the Oxford and
the Chicago schools.[18] I can not, however, be sure that all
these doctrines are its necessary and indispensable allies. It
presents so many points of difference, both from the common sense and from the idealism that have made our philosophic language, that it is almost as difficult to state it as it
is to think it out clearly, and if it is ever to grow into a
respectable system, it will have to be built up by the contri-
butions of many co-operating minds. It seems to me, as I
said at the outset of this essay, that many minds are, in
point of fact, now turning in a direction that points towards
radical empiricism. If they are carried farther by my words,
and if then they add their stronger voices to my feebler one,
the publication of this essay will have been worth while.

---

[18] I have said something of this latter alliance in an article entitled
"Humanism and Truth," in *Mind,* October, 1904. [Reprinted in *The
Meaning of Truth,* pp. 51–101. Cf. also essay XI below, "Humanism and
Truth Once More."]

III
THE THING AND ITS RELATIONS[1]

Experience in its immediacy seems perfectly fluent. The active sense of living which we all enjoy, before reflection shatters our instinctive world for us, is self-luminous and suggests no paradoxes. Its difficulties are disappointments and uncertainties. They are not intellectual contradictions.

When the reflective intellect gets at work, however, it discovers incomprehensibilities in the flowing process. Distinguishing its elements and parts, it gives them separate names, and what it thus disjoins it can not easily put together. Pyrrhonism accepts the irrationality and revels in its dialectic elaboration. Other philosophies try, some by ignoring, some by resisting, and some by turning the dialectic procedure against itself, negating its first negations, to restore the fluent sense of life again, and let redemption take the place of innocence. The perfection with which any philosophy may do this is the measure of its human success and of its importance in philosophic history. In [the last essay], "A World of Pure Experience," I tried my own hand sketchily at the problem, resisting certain first steps of dialectics by insisting in a general way that the immediately experienced conjunctive relations are as real as anything else. If my sketch is not to appear too *naïf*, I must come closer to details, and in the present essay I propose to do so.

---

[1] [Reprinted from *The Journal of Philosophy, Psychology and Scientific Methods,* vol. II, No. 2, January 19, 1905. Reprinted also as Appendix A in *A Pluralistic Universe*. The author's corrections have been adopted in the present text. ED.]

I

"Pure experience" is the name which I gave to the immediate flux of life which furnishes the material to our later
reflection with its conceptual categories. Only new-born
babes, or men in semi-coma from sleep, drugs, illnesses, or
blows, may be assumed to have an experience pure in the
literal sense of a *that* which is not yet any definite *what,*
tho' ready to be all sorts of whats; full both of oneness and
of manyness, but in respects that don't appear; changing
throughout, yet so confusedly that its phases interpenetrate
and no points, either of distinction or of identity, can be
caught. Pure experience in this state is but another name
for feeling or sensation. But the flux of it no sooner comes
than it tends to fill itself with emphases, and these salient
parts become identified and fixed and abstracted; so that
experience now flows as if shot through with adjectives and
nouns and prepositions and conjunctions. Its purity is only
a relative term, meaning the proportional amount of unver-
balized sensation which it still embodies.

Far back as we go, the flux, both as a whole and in its
parts, is that of things conjunct and separated. The great
continua of time, space, and the self envelop everything,
betwixt them, and flow together without interfering. The
things that they envelop come as separate in some ways
and as continuous in others. Some sensations coalesce with
some ideas, and others are irreconcilable. Qualities compenetrate one space, or exclude each other from it. They
cling together persistently in groups that move as units, or
else they separate. Their changes are abrupt or discontinuous; and their kinds resemble or differ; and, as they do so,
they fall into either even or irregular series.

In all this the continuities and the discontinuities are
absolutely co-ordinate matters of immediate feeling. The
conjunctions are as primordial elements of "fact" as are the
distinctions and disjunctions. In the same act by which I
feel that this passing minute is a new pulse of my life, I feel
that the old life continues into it, and the feeling of contin-

uance in no wise jars upon the simultaneous feeling of a novelty. They, too, compenetrate harmoniously. Prepositions, copulas, and conjunctions, "is," "isn't," "then," "before," "in," "on," "beside," "between," "next," "like," "unlike," "as," "but," flower out of the stream of pure experience, the stream of concretes or the sensational stream, as naturally as nouns and adjectives do, and they melt into it again as fluidly when we apply them to a new portion of the stream.

II

If now we ask why we must thus translate experience from a more concrete or pure into a more intellectualized form, filling it with ever more abounding conceptual distinctions, rationalism and naturalism give different replies.

The rationalistic answer is that the theoretic life is absolute and its interests imperative; that to understand is simply the duty of man; and that who questions this need not be argued with, for by the fact of arguing he gives away his case.

The naturalist answer is that the environment kills as well as sustains us, and that the tendency of raw experience to extinguish the experient himself is lessened just in the degree in which the elements in it that have a practical bearing upon life are analyzed out of the continuum and verbally fixed and coupled together, so that we may know what is in the wind for us and get ready to react in time. Had pure experience, the naturalist says, been always perfectly healthy, there would never have arisen the necessity of isolating or verbalizing any of its terms. We should just have experienced inarticulately and unintellectually enjoyed. This leaning on "reaction" in the naturalist account implies that, whenever we intellectualize a relatively pure experience, we ought to do so for the sake of redescending to the purer or more concrete level again; and that if an intellect stays aloft among its abstract terms and generalized relations, and does not reinsert itself with its conclusions into some particular point of the immediate stream of life, it fails to finish out its function and leaves its normal race unrun.

Most rationalists nowadays will agree that naturalism gives a true enough account of the way in which our intellect arose at first, but they will deny these latter implications. The case, they will say, resembles that of sexual love. Originating in the animal need of getting another generation born, this passion has developed secondarily such imperious spiritual needs that, if you ask why another generation ought to be born at all, the answer is: "Chiefly that love may go on." Just so with our intellect: it originated as a practical means of serving life; but it has developed incidentally the function of understanding absolute truth; and life itself now seems to be given chiefly as a means by which that function may be prosecuted. But truth and the understanding of it lie among the abstracts and universals, so the intellect now carries on its higher business wholly in this region, without any need of redescending into pure experience again.

If the contrasted tendencies which I thus designate as naturalistic and rationalistic are not recognized by the reader, perhaps an example will make them more concrete. Mr. Bradley, for instance, is an ultra-rationalist. He admits that our intellect is primarily practical, but says that, for philosophers, the practical need is simply Truth. Truth, moreover, must be assumed "consistent." Immediate experience has to be broken into subjects and qualities, terms and relations, to be understood as truth at all. Yet when so broken it is less consistent than ever. Taken raw, it is all undistinguished. Intellectualized, it is all distinction without oneness. "Such an arrangement may *work,* but the theoretic problem is not solved." The question is "*how* the diversity can exist in harmony with the oneness." To go back to pure experience is unavailing. "Mere feeling gives no answer to our riddle." Even if your intuition is a fact, it is not an *understanding.* "It is a mere experience, and furnishes no consistent view." The experience offered as facts or truths "I find that my intellect rejects because they con-

tradict themselves. They offer a complex of diversities conjoined in a way which it feels is not its way and which it can
not repeat as its own. . . . For to be satisfied, my intellect
must understand, and it can not understand by taking a
congeries in the lump."[2] So Mr. Bradley, in the sole interests
of "understanding" (as he conceives that function), turns his
back on finite experience forever. Truth must lie in the
opposite direction, the direction of the Absolute; and this
kind of rationalism and naturalism, or (as I will now call it)
pragmatism, walk thenceforward upon opposite paths. For
the one, those intellectual products are most true which,
turning their face towards the Absolute, come nearest to
symbolizing its ways of uniting the many and the one. For
the other, those are most true which most successfully dip
back into the finite stream of feeling and grow most easily
confluent with some particular wave or wavelet. Such confluence not only proves the intellectual operation to have
been true (as an addition may "prove" that a subtraction is
already rightly performed), but it constitutes, according to
pragmatism, all that we mean by calling it true. Only in so
far as they lead us, successfully or unsuccessfully, back into
sensible experience again, are our abstracts and universals
true or false at all.[3]

III

In Section VI of [the last essay], I adopted in a general
way the common-sense belief that one and the same world
is cognized by our different minds; but I left undiscussed
the dialectical arguments which maintain that this is logically absurd. The usual reason given for its being absurd is
that it assumes one object (to wit, the world) to stand in two
relations at once; to my mind, namely, and again to yours;

---

[2] [F. H. Bradley: *Appearance and Reality,* second edition, pp. 152–153, 23,
118, 104, 108–109, 570.]
[3] Compare Professor MacLennan's admirable *Auseinandersetzung* with
Mr. Bradley, in *The Journal of Philosophy, Psychology and Scientific
Methods,* vol. I, [1904], pp. 403 ff., especially pp. 405–407.

whereas a term taken in a second relation can not logically be the same term which it was at first.

I have heard this reason urged so often in discussing with absolutists, and it would destroy my radical empiricism so utterly, if it were valid, that I am bound to give it an attentive ear, and seriously to search its strength.

For instance, let the matter in dispute be term M, asserted to be on the one hand related to L, and on the other to N; and let the two cases of relation be symbolized by L—M and M—N respectively. When, now, I assume that the experience may immediately come and be given in the shape L—M—N, with no trace of doubling or internal fission in the M, I am told that this is all a popular delusion; that L—M—N logically means two different experiences, L—M and M—N, namely; and that although the Absolute may, and indeed must, from its superior point of view, read its own kind of unity into M's two editions, yet as elements in finite experience the two M's lie irretrievably asunder, and the world between them is broken and unbridged.

In arguing this dialectic thesis, one must avoid slipping from the logical into the physical point of view. It would be easy, in taking a concrete example to fix one's ideas by, to choose one in which the letter M should stand for a collective noun of some sort, which noun, being related to L by one of its parts and to N by another, would inwardly be two things when it stood outwardly in both relations. Thus, one might say: "David Hume, who weighed so many stone by his body, influences posterity by his doctrine." The body and the doctrine are two things, between which our finite minds can discover no real sameness, though the same name covers both of them. And then, one might continue: "Only an Absolute is capable of uniting such a non-identity." We must, I say, avoid this sort of example, for the dialectic insight, if true at all, must apply to terms and relations universally. It must be true of abstract units as well as of nouns collective; and if we prove it by concrete examples we must take the simplest, so as to avoid irrelevant material suggestions.

Taken thus in all its generality, the absolutist contention seems to use as its major premise Hume's notion "that all our distinct perceptions are distinct existences, and that the mind never perceives any real connection among distinct existences."[4] Undoubtedly, since we use two phrases in talking first about "M's relation to L" and then about "M's relation to N," we must be having, or must have had, two distinct perceptions;—and the rest would then seem to follow duly. But the starting-point of the reasoning here seems to be the fact of the two *phrases;* and this suggests that the argument may be merely verbal. Can it be that the whole dialectic consists in attributing to the experience talked-about a constitution similar to that of the language in which we describe it? Must we assert the objective doubleness of the M merely because we have to name it twice over when we name its two relations?

Candidly, I can think of no other reason than this for the dialectic conclusion;[5] for, if we think, not of our words, but of any simple concrete matter which they may be held to signify, the experience itself belies the paradox asserted. We use indeed two separate concepts in analyzing our object, but we know them all the while to be but substitutional, and that the M in $L—M$ and the M in $M—N$ *mean* (i.e., are capable of leading to and terminating in) one self-same piece, $M,$ of sensible experience. This persistent identity of certain units (or emphases, or points, or objects, or members—call them what you will) of the experience-continuum, is just one of those conjunctive features of it, on which I am obliged to insist so emphatically.[6] For same-nesses are parts of experience's indefeasible structure. When I hear a bell-stroke and, as life flows on, its after image dies away, I still hark back to it as "that same bell-

---

[4] [Hume: *Treatise of Human Nature,* Appendix, Selby-Bigge's edition, p. 636.]

[5] Technically, it seems classable as a "fallacy of composition." A duality, predicable of the two wholes, $L—M$ and $M—N,$ is forthwith predicated of one of their parts, $M.$

[6] See above, pp. 22 ff.

stroke." When I see a thing *M,* with *L* to the left of it and *N* to the right of it, I see it *as* one *M;* and if you tell me I have had to "take" it twice, I reply that if I "took" it a thousand times I should still *see* it as a unit.[7] Its unity is aboriginal, just as the multiplicity of my successive takings is aboriginal. It comes unbroken as *that M,* as a singular which I encounter; they come broken, as *those* takings, as my plurality of operations. The unity and the separateness are strictly co-ordinate. I do not easily fathom why my opponents should find the separateness so much more easily understandable that they must needs infect the whole of finite experience with it, and relegate the unity (now taken as a bare postulate and no longer as a thing positively perceivable) to the region of the Absolute's mysteries. I do not easily fathom this, I say, for the said opponents are above mere verbal quibbling; yet all that I can catch in their talk is the substitution of what is true of certain words for what is true of what they signify. They stay with the words,—not returning to the stream of life whence all the meaning of them came, and which is always ready to reabsorb them.

IV

For aught this argument proves, then, we may continue to believe that one thing can be known by many knowers. But the denial of one thing in many relations is but one application of a still profounder dialectic difficulty. Man can't be good, said the sophists, for man is *man* and *good* is good; and Hegel[8] and Herbart in their day, more recently A. Spir,[9] and most recently and elaborately of all, Mr. Bradley, informs us

---

[7] I may perhaps refer here to my *Principles of Psychology,* vol. I, pp. 459 ff. It really seems "weird" to have to argue (as I am forced now to do) for the notion that it is one sheet of paper (with its two surfaces and all that lies between) which is both under my pen and on the table while I write—the "claim" that it is two sheets seems so brazen. Yet I sometimes suspect the absolutists of sincerity!

[8] [For the author's criticism of Hegel's view of relations, cf. *Will to Believe,* pp. 278–279. ED.]

[9] [Cf. A. Spir: *Denken und Wirklichkeit,* part I, bk. III, ch. IV (containing also account of Herbart). ED.]

that a term can logically only be a punctiform unit, and that not one of the conjunctive relations between things, which experience seems to yield, is rationally possible.

Of course, if true, this cuts off radical empiricism without even a shilling. Radical empiricism takes conjunctive relations at their face value, holding them to be as real as the terms united by them. The world it represents as a collection, some parts of which are conjunctively and others disjunctively related. Two parts, themselves disjoined, may nevertheless hang together by intermediaries with which they are severally connected, and the whole world eventually may hang together similarly, inasmuch as *some* path of conjunctive transition by which to pass from one of its parts to another may always be discernible. Such determinately various hanging-together may be called *concatenated* union, to distinguish it from the "through-and-through" type of union, "each in all and all in each" (union of *total conflux,* as one might call it), which monistic systems hold to obtain when things are taken in their absolute reality. In a concatenated world a partial conflux often is experienced. Our concepts and our sensations are confluent; successive states of the same ego, and feelings of the same body are confluent. Where the experience is not of conflux, it may be of conterminousness (things with but one thing between); or of contiguousness (nothing between); or of likeness; or of nearness; or of simultaneousness; or of in-ness; or of on-ness; or of for-ness; or of simple with-ness; or even of mere and-ness, which last relation would make of however disjointed a world otherwise, at any rate for that occasion a universe "of discourse." Now Mr. Bradley tells us that none of these relations, as we actually experience them, can possibly be real.[10] My next duty, accordingly, must be to rescue

---

[10] Here again the reader must beware of slipping from logical into phenomenal considerations. It may well be that we *attribute* a certain relation falsely, because the circumstances of the case, being complex, have deceived us. At a railway station we may take our own train, and not the one that fills our window, to be moving. We here put motion in the wrong place in the world, but in its original place the motion is a part

radical empiricism from Mr. Bradley. Fortunately, as it seems to me, his general contention, that the very notion of relation is unthinkable clearly, has been successfully met by many critics.[11]

It is a burden to the flesh, and an injustice both to readers and to the previous writers, to repeat good arguments already printed. So, in noticing Mr. Bradley, I will confine myself to the interests of radical empiricism solely.

V

The first duty of radical empiricism, taking given conjunctions at their face-value, is to class some of them as more intimate and some as more external. When two terms are *similar,* their very natures enter into the relation. Being *what* they are, no matter where or when, the likeness never can be denied, if asserted. It continues predictable as long as the terms continue. Other relations, the *where* and the *when,* for example, seem adventitious. The sheet of paper may be "off" or "on" the table, for example; and in either case the relation involves only the outside of its terms. Having an outside, both of them, they contribute by it to the relation. It is external: the term's inner nature is irrelevant to it. Any book, any table, may fall into the relation, which is created *pro hac vice,* not by their existence, but by their casual situation. It is just because so many of the conjunctions of experience seem so external that a philosophy of pure experience must tend to pluralism in its ontology. So far as things have space-relations, for example, we are free to imagine them with different origins even. If

---

of reality. What Mr. Bradley means is nothing like this, but rather that such things as motion are nowhere real, and that, even in their aboriginal and empirically incorrigible seats, relations are impossible of comprehension.

[11] Particularly so by Andrew Seth Pringle-Pattison, in his *Man and the Cosmos;* by L. T. Hobhouse, in chapter XII ("The Validity of Judgment") of his *Theory of Knowledge;* and by F. C. S. Schiller, in his *Humanism,* essay XI. Other fatal reviews (in my opinion) are Hodder's, in the *Psychological Review,* vol. I [1894], p. 307; Stout's in the *Proceedings of the Aristotelian Society,* 1901–2, p. 1; and MacLennan's in [*The Journal of Philosophy, Psychology and Scientific Methods,* vol. I, 1904, p. 403].

they could get to *be,* and get into space at all, then they may have done so separately. Once there, however, they are *additives* to one another, and, with no prejudice to their natures, all sorts of space-relations may supervene between them. The question of how things could come to be anyhow, is wholly different from the question what their relations, once the being accomplished, may consist in.

Mr. Bradley now affirms that such external relations as the space-relations which we here talk of must hold of entirely different subjects from those of which the absence of such relations might a moment previously have been plausibly asserted. Not only is the *situation* different when the book is on the table, but the *book itself* is different as a book, from what it was when it was off the table.[12] He admits that "such external relations seem possible and even existing. . . . That you do not alter what you compare or rearrange in space seems to common sense quite obvious, and that on the other side there are as obvious difficulties does not occur to common sense at all. And I will begin by pointing out these difficulties. . . . There is a relation in the result, and this relation, we hear, is to make no difference in its terms. But, if so, to what does it make a difference? [*Doesn't it make a difference to us on-lookers, at least?*] and what is the meaning and sense of qualifying the terms by it? [*Surely the meaning is to tell the truth about their relative position.*[13]] If, in short, it is external to the terms, how

---

[12] Once more, don't slip from logical into physical situations. Of course, if the table be wet, it will moisten the book, or if it be slight enough and the book heavy enough, the book will break it down. But such collateral phenomena are not the point at issue. The point is whether the successive relations "on" and "not-on" can rationally (not physically) hold of the same constant terms, abstractly taken. Professor A. E. Taylor drops from logical into material considerations when he instances color-contrast as a proof that *A,* "as contra-distinguished from *B,* is not the same thing as mere *A* not in any way affected" (*Elements of Metaphysics,* p. 145). Note the substitution, for "related" of the word "affected," which begs the whole question.

[13] But "is there any sense," asks Mr. Bradley, peevishly, on p. 579, "and if so, what sense in truth that is only outside and 'about' things?" Surely such a question may be left unanswered.

can it possibly be true *of* them? [*Is it the "intimacy" suggested by the little word "of," here, which I have underscored, that is the root of Mr. Bradley's trouble?*] . . . If the terms from their inner nature do not enter into the relation, then, so far as they are concerned, they seem related for no reason at all. . . . Things are spatially related, first in one way, and then become related in another way, and yet in no way themselves are altered; for the relations, it is said, are but external. But I reply that, if so, I can not *understand* the leaving by the terms of one set of relations and their adoption of another fresh set. The process and its result to the terms, if they contribute nothing to it [*Surely they contribute to it all there is "of" it!*] seem irrational throughout. [*If "irrational" here means simply "non-rational," or non-deducible from the essence of either term singly, it is no reproach; if it means "contradicting" such essence, Mr. Bradley should show wherein and how.*] But, if they contribute anything, they must surely be affected internally. [*Why so, if they contribute only their surface? In such relations as "on," "a foot away," "between," "next," etc., only surfaces are in question.*] . . . If the terms contribute anything whatever, then the terms are affected [*inwardly altered?*] by the arrangement. . . . That for working purposes we treat, and do well to treat, some relations as external merely I do not deny, and that of course is not the question at issue here. That question is . . . whether in the end and in principle a mere external relation [*i.e., a relation which can change without forcing its terms to change their nature simultaneously*] is possible and forced on us by the facts."[14]

Mr. Bradley next reverts to the antinomies of space, which, according to him, prove it to be unreal, although it appears as so prolific a medium of external relations; and he then concludes that "Irrationality and externality can not be the last truth about things. Somewhere there must be a reason why this and that appear together. And this reason and reality must reside in the whole from which terms and relations are

---

[14] *Appearance and Reality,* second edition, pp. 575–576.

abstractions, a whole in which their internal connection must lie, and out of which from the background appear those fresh results which never could have come from the premises." And he adds that "Where the whole is different, the terms that qualify and contribute to it must so far be different. . . . They are altered so far only [*How far? farther than externally, yet not through and through?*] but still they are altered. . . . I must insist that in each case the terms are qualified by their whole [*Qualified how?—Do their external relations, situations, dates, etc., changed as these are in the new whole, fail to qualify them "far" enough?*], and that in the second case there is a whole which differs both logically and psychologically from the first whole; and I urge that in contributing to the change the terms so far are altered."

Not merely the relations, then, but the terms are altered: *und zwar* "so far." But just *how* far is the whole problem; and "through-and-through" would seem (in spite of Mr. Bradley's somewhat undecided utterances[15]) to be the full Bradleyan answer. The "whole" which he here treats as primary and determinative of each part's manner of "contributing," simply *must,* when it alters, alter in its entirety.

---

[15] I say "undecided," because, apart from the "so far," which sounds terribly half-hearted, there are passages in these very pages in which Mr. Bradley admits the pluralistic thesis. Read, for example, what he says, on p. 578, of a billiard ball keeping its "character" unchanged, though, in its change of place, its "existence" gets altered; or what he says, on p. 579, of the possibility that an abstract quality A, B, or C, in a thing, "may throughout remain unchanged" although the thing be altered; or his admission that in red-hairedness, both as analyzed out of a man and when given with the rest of him, there may be "no change" (p. 580). Why does he immediately add that for the pluralist to plead the non-mutation of such abstractions would be an *ignoratio elenchi?* It is impossible to admit it to be such. The entire *elenchus* and inquest is just as to whether parts which you can abstract from existing wholes can also contribute to other wholes without changing their inner nature. If they can thus mold various wholes into new *gestaltqualitäten,* then it follows that the same elements are logically able to exist in different wholes [whether physically able would depend on additional hypotheses]; that partial changes are thinkable, and through-and-through change not a dialectic necessity; that monism is only an hypothesis; and that an additively constituted universe is a rationally respectable hypothesis also. All the theses of radical empiricism, in short, follow.

There *must* be total conflux of its parts, each into and through each other. The "must" appears here as a *Machtspruch,* as an *ipse dixit* of Mr. Bradley's absolutistically tempered "understanding," for he candidly confesses that how the parts *do* differ as they contribute to different wholes, is unknown to him.[16]

Although I have every wish to comprehend the authority by which Mr. Bradley's understanding speaks, his words leave me wholly unconverted. "External relations" stand with their withers all unwrung, and remain, for aught he proves to the contrary, not only practically workable, but also perfectly intelligible factors of reality.

VI

Mr. Bradley's understanding shows the most extraordinary power of perceiving separations and the most extraordinary impotence in comprehending conjunctions. One would naturally say "neither or both," but not so Mr. Bradley. When a common man analyzes certain *whats* from out the stream of experience, he understands their distinctness *as thus isolated.* But this does not prevent him from equally well understanding their combination with each other *as originally experienced in the concrete,* or their confluence with new sensible experiences in which they recur as "the same." Returning into the stream of sensible presentation, nouns and adjectives, and *thats* and abstract *whats,* grow confluent again, and the word "is" names all these experiences of conjunction. Mr. Bradley understands the isolation of the abstracts, but to understand the combination is to him impossible.[17] "To understand a complex

---

[16] *Op. cit.,* pp. 577–579.

[17] So far as I catch his state of mind, it is somewhat like this: "Book," "table," "on"—how does the existence of these three abstract elements result in *this* book being livingly on *this* table. Why isn't the table on the book? Or why doesn't the "on" connect itself with another book, or something that is not a table? Mustn't something *in* each of the three elements already determine the two others to *it,* so that they do not settle elsewhere or float vaguely? Mustn't the *whole fact be prefigured in each part,* and exist *de jure* before it can exist *de facto*? But, if so, in what can

AB," he says, "I must begin with *A* or *B*. And beginning, say with *A*, if I then merely find *B*, I have either lost *A*, or I have got beside *A*, [*the word "beside" seems here vital, as meaning a conjunction "external" and therefore unintelligible*] something else, and in neither case have I understood.[18] For my intellect can not simply unite a diversity, nor has it in itself any form or way of togetherness, and you gain nothing if, beside *A* and *B*, you offer me their conjunction in fact. For to my intellect that is no more than another external element. And 'facts,' once for all, are for my intellect not true unless they satisfy it. . . . The intellect has in its nature no principle of mere togetherness."[19]

Of course Mr. Bradley has a right to define "intellect" as the power by which we perceive separations but not unions—provided he give due notice to the reader. But why then claim that such a maimed and amputated power must reign supreme in philosophy, and accuse on its behoof the whole empirical world of irrationality? It is true that he elsewhere attributes to the intellect a *proprius motus* of transition, but says that when he looks for *these* transitions in the detail of living experience, he "is unable to verify such a solution."[20]

Yet he never explains what the intellectual transitions would be like in case we had them. He only defines them negatively—they are not spatial, temporal, predicative, or causal; or qualitatively or otherwise serial; or in any way relational as we naïvely trace relations, for relations *separate* terms, and need themselves to be hooked on *ad infinitum*. The nearest approach he makes to describing a truly intellectual transition is where he speaks of *A* and *B* as

---

the jural existence consist, if not in a spiritual miniature of the whole fact's constitution actuating every partial factor as its purpose? But is this anything but the old metaphysical fallacy of looking behind a fact *in esse* for the ground of the fact, and finding it in the shape of the very same fact *in posse?* Somewhere we must leave off with a *constitution* behind which there is nothing.

[18] Apply this to the case of "book-on-table"! W. J.

[19] *Op. cit.*, pp. 570, 572.

[20] *Op. cit.*, pp. 568, 569.

being "united, each from its own nature, in a whole which is the nature of both alike."[21] But this (which, *pace* Mr. Bradley, seems exquisitely analogous to "taking" a congeries in a "lump," if not to "swamping") suggests nothing but that *conflux* which pure experience so abundantly offers, as when "space," "white" and "sweet" are confluent in a "lump of sugar," or kinesthetic, dermal, and optical sensations confluent in "my hand."[22] All that I can verify in the transitions which Mr. Bradley's intellect desiderates as its *proprius motus* is a reminiscence of these and other sensible conjunctions (especially space-conjunctions), but a reminiscence so vague that its originals are not recognized. Bradley in short repeats the fable of the dog, the bone, and its image in the water. With a world of particulars, given in loveliest union, in conjunction definitely various, and variously definite, the "how" of which you "understand" as soon as you see the fact of them,[23] for there is no "how" except the constitution of the fact as given; with all this given him, I say, in pure experience, he asks for some ineffable union in the abstract instead, which, if he gained it, would only be a duplicate of what he has already in his full possession. Surely he abuses the privilege which society grants to all us philosophers, of being puzzle-headed.

Polemic writing like this is odious; but with absolutism in possession in so many quarters, omission to defend my radical empiricism against its best known champion would count as either superficiality or inability. I have to conclude that its dialectic has not invalidated in the least degree the usual conjunctions by which the world, as experienced, hangs so variously together. In particular it leaves an

---

[21] *Op. cit.*, p. 570.

[22] How meaningless is the contention that in such wholes (or in "book-on-table," "watch-in-pocket," etc.) the relation is an additional entity *between* the terms, needing itself to be related again to each! Both Bradley (*op. cit.*, pp. 32–33) and Royce (*The World and the Individual*, vol. I, p. 128) lovingly repeat this piece of profundity.

[23] The "why" and the "whence" are entirely other questions, not under discussion, as I understand Mr. Bradley. Not how experience gets itself born, but how it can be what it is after it is born, is the puzzle.

empirical theory of knowledge[24] intact, and lets us continue to believe with common sense that one object *may* be known, if we have any ground for thinking that it *is* known, to many knowers.

In [the next essay] I shall return to this last supposition, which seems to me to offer other difficulties much harder for a philosophy of pure experience to deal with than any of absolutism's dialectic objections.

---

[24] Above, pp. 27–28.

IV
How Two Minds Can Know One Thing[1]

In [the essay] entitled "Does 'Consciousness' Exist?" I have tried to show that when we call an experience "conscious," that does not mean that it is suffused throughout with a peculiar modality of being ("psychic" being) as stained glass may be suffused with light, but rather that it stands in certain determinate relations to other portions of experience extraneous to itself. These form one peculiar "context" for it; while, taken in another context of experiences, we class it as a fact in the physical world. This "pen," for example, is, in the first instance, a bald *that,* a datum, fact, phenomenon, content, or whatever other neutral or ambiguous name you may prefer to apply. I called it in that article a "pure experience." To get classed either as a physical pen or as some one's percept of a pen, it must assume a *function,* and that can only happen in a more complicated world. So far as in that world it is a stable feature, holds ink, marks paper and obeys the guidance of a hand, it is a physical pen. That is what we mean by being "physical," in a pen. So far as it is instable, on the contrary, coming and going with the movements of my eyes, altering with what I call my fancy, continuous with subsequent experiences of its "having been" (in the past tense), it is the percept of a pen in my mind. Those peculiarities are what we mean by being "conscious," in a pen.

In Section VI of another [essay][2] I tried to show that the

---

[1] [Reprinted from *The Journal of Philosophy, Psychology and Scientific Methods,* vol. II, No. 7, March 30, 1905.]
[2] "A World of Pure Experience," above.

same *that,* the same numerically identical pen of pure experience, can enter simultaneously into many conscious contexts, or, in other words, be an object for many different
minds. I admitted that I had not space to treat of certain
possible objections in that article; but in [the last essay] I
took some of the objections up. At the end of that [essay] I
said that still more formidable-sounding objections
remained; so, to leave my pure-experience theory in as
strong a state as possible, I propose to consider those objections now.

I

The objections I previously tried to dispose of were purely
logical or dialectical. No one identical term, whether physical or psychical, it had been said, could be the subject of two
relations at once. This thesis I sought to prove unfounded.
The objections that now confront us arise from the nature
supposed to inhere in psychic facts specifically. Whatever
may be the case with physical objects, a fact of consciousness, it is alleged (and indeed very plausibly), can not, without self-contradiction, be treated as a portion of two different minds, and for the following reasons.

In the physical world we make with impunity the
assumption that one and the same material object can figure in an indefinitely large number of different processes at
once. When, for instance, a sheet of rubber is pulled at its
four corners, a unit of rubber in the middle of the sheet is
affected by all four of the pulls. It *transmits* them each, as
if it pulled in four different ways at once itself. So, an air-
particle or an ether-particle "compounds" the different
directions of movement imprinted on it without obliterating
their several individualities. It delivers them distinct, on
the contrary, at as many several "receivers" (ear, eye or
what not) as may be "tuned" to that effect. The apparent
paradox of a distinctness like this surviving in the midst of
compounding is a thing which, I fancy, the analyses made
by physicists have by this time sufficiently cleared up.

But if, on the strength of these analogies, one should ask:

"Why, if two or more lines can run through one and the same geometrical point, or if two or more distinct processes of activity can run through one and the same physical thing so that it simultaneously plays a rôle in each and every process, might not two or more streams of personal consciousness include one and the same unit of experience so that it would simultaneously be a part of the experience of all the different minds?" one would be checked by thinking of a certain peculiarity by which phenomena of consciousness differ from physical things.

While physical things, namely, are supposed to be permanent and to have their "states," a fact of consciousness exists but once and *is* a state. Its *esse* is *sentiri;* it is only so far as it is felt; and it is unambiguously and unequivocally exactly *what* is felt. The hypothesis under consideration would, however, oblige it to be felt equivocally, felt now as part of my mind and again at the same time *not* as a part of my mind, but of yours (for my mind is *not* yours), and this would seem impossible without doubling it into two distinct things, or, in other words, without reverting to the ordinary dualistic philosophy of insulated minds each knowing its object representatively as a third thing,—and that would be to give up the pure-experience scheme altogether.

Can we see, then, any way in which a unit of pure experience might enter into and figure in two diverse streams of consciousness without turning itself into the two units which, on our hypothesis, it must not be?

II

There is a way; and the first step towards it is to see more precisely how the unit enters into either one of the streams of consciousness alone. Just what, from being "pure," does its becoming "conscious" *once* mean?

It means, first, that new experiences have supervened; and, second, that they have borne a certain assignable relation to the unit supposed. Continue, if you please, to speak of the pure unit as "the pen." So far as the pen's successors do but repeat the pen or, being different from it, are "energetically"[3] related to it, it and they will form a group of stably existing physical things. So far, however, as its successors differ from it in another well-determined way, the pen will figure in their context, not as a physical, but as a mental fact. It will become a passing "percept," *my* percept of that pen. What now is that decisive well-determined way?

In the chapter on "The Self," in my *Principles of Psychology,* I explained the continuous identity of each personal consciousness as a name for the practical fact that new experiences[4] come which look back on the old ones, find them "warm," and greet and appropriate them as "mine." These operations mean, when analyzed empirically, several tolerably definite things, viz.:

1. That the new experience has past time for its "content," and in that time a pen that "was";

2. That "warmth" was also about the pen, in the sense of a group of feelings ("interest" aroused, "attention" turned, "eyes" employed, etc.) that were closely connected with it and that now recur and evermore recur with unbroken vividness, though from the pen of now, which may be only an image, all such vividness may have gone;

3. That these feelings are the nucleus of "me";

4. That whatever once was associated with them was, at least for that one moment, "mine"—my implement if associated with hand-feelings, my "percept" only, if only eye-feelings and attention-feelings were involved.

The pen, realized in this retrospective way as my percept, thus figures as a fact of "conscious" life. But it does so only so far as "appropriation" has occurred; and appropriation is *part of the content of a later experience* wholly additional to the originally "pure" pen. *That* pen, virtually both objective and subjective, is at its own moment actually and intrinsically neither. It has to be looked back upon and *used,* in order to be classed in either distinctive way. But its use, so

---

[3] [For an explanation of this expression, see essay I above, "Does 'Consciousness' Exist?" §VI.]

[4] I call them "passing thoughts" in the book—the passage in point goes from pages 330 to 342 of vol. I.

called, is in the hands of the other experience, while *it* stands, throughout the operation, passive and unchanged.

If this pass muster as an intelligible account of how an experience originally pure can enter into one consciousness, the next question is as to how it might conceivably enter into two.

III

Obviously no new kind of condition would have to be supplied. All that we should have to postulate would be a second subsequent experience, collateral and contemporary with the first subsequent one, in which a similar act of appropriation should occur. The two acts would interfere neither with one another nor with the originally pure pen. It would sleep undisturbed in its own past, no matter how many such successors went through their several appropriative acts. Each would know it as "my" percept, each would class it as a "conscious" fact.

Nor need their so classing it interfere in the least with their classing it at the same time as a physical pen. Since the classing in both cases depends upon the taking of it in one group or another of associates, if the superseding experience were of wide enough "span" it could think the pen in both groups simultaneously, and yet distinguish the two groups. It would then see the whole situation conformably to what we call "the representative theory of cognition," and that is what we all spontaneously do. As a man philosophizing "popularly," I believe that what I see myself writing with is double—I think it in its relations to physical nature, and also in its relations to my personal life; I see that it is in my mind, but that it also is a physical pen.

The paradox of the same experience figuring in two consciousnesses seems thus no paradox at all. To be "conscious" means not simply to be, but to be reported, known, to have awareness of one's being added to that being; and this is just what happens when the appropriative experience supervenes. The pen-experience in its original immediacy is not aware of itself, it simply *is,* and the second experience is required for what we call awareness of it to occur.[5] The difficulty of understanding what happens here is, therefore, not a logical difficulty: there is no contradiction involved. It is an ontological difficulty rather. Experiences come on an enormous scale, and if we take them all together, they come in a chaos of incommensurable relations that we can not straighten out. We have to abstract different groups of them, and handle these separately if we are to talk of them at all. But how the experiences ever *get themselves made,* or *why* their characters and relations are just such as appear, we can not begin to understand. Granting, however, that, by hook or crook, they *can* get themselves made, and can appear in the successions that I have so schematically described, then we have to confess that even although (as I began by quoting from the adversary) "a feeling only is as it is felt," there is still nothing absurd in the notion of its being felt in two different ways at once, as yours, namely, and as mine. It is, indeed, "mine" only as it is felt as mine, and "yours" only as it is felt as yours. But it is felt as neither *by itself,* but only when "owned" by our two several remembering experiences, just as one undivided estate is owned by several heirs.

IV

One word, now, before I close, about the corollaries of the view set forth. Since the acquisition of conscious quality on the part of an experience depends upon a context coming to it, it follows that the sum total of all experiences, having no context, can not strictly be called conscious at all. It is a *that,* an Absolute, a "pure" experience on an enormous scale, undifferentiated and undifferentiable into thought

---

[5] Shadworth Hodgson has laid great stress on the fact that the minimum of consciousness demands two subfeelings, of which the second retrospects the first. (Cf. the section "Analysis of Minima" in his *Philosophy of Reflection,* vol. I, p. 248; also the chapter entitled "The Moment of Experience" in his *Metaphysic of Experience,* vol. I, p. 34.) "We live forward, but we understand backward" is a phrase of Kierkegaard's which Höffding quotes. [H. Höffding: "A Philosophical Confession," *Journal of Philosophy, Psychology and Scientific Methods,* vol. II, 1905, p. 86.]

and thing. This the post-Kantian idealists have always practically acknowledged by calling their doctrine an *Identitätsphilosophie*. The question of the *Beseelung* of the All of things ought not, then, even to be asked. No more ought the question of its *truth* to be asked, for truth is a relation inside of the sum total, obtaining between thoughts and something else, and thoughts, as we have seen, can only be contextual things. In these respects the pure experiences of our philosophy are, in themselves considered, so many little absolutes, the philosophy of pure experience being only a more comminuted *Identitätsphilosophie*.

Meanwhile, a pure experience can be postulated with any amount whatever of span or field. If it exert the retrospective and appropriative function on any other piece of experience, the latter thereby enters into its own conscious stream. And in this operation time intervals make no essential difference. After sleeping, my retrospection is as perfect as it is between two successive waking moments of my time. Accordingly if, millions of years later, a similarly retrospective experience should anyhow come to birth, my present thought would form a genuine portion of its long-span conscious life. "Form a portion," I say, but not in the sense that the two things could be entitatively or substantively one— they cannot, for they are numerically discrete facts—but only in the sense that the *functions* of my present thought, its knowledge, its purpose, its content and "consciousness," in short, being inherited, would be continued practically unchanged. Speculations like Fechner's, of an Earth-soul, of wider spans of consciousness enveloping narrower ones throughout the cosmos, are, therefore, philosophically quite in order, provided they distinguish the functional from the entitative point of view, and do not treat the minor consciousness under discussion as a kind of standing material of which the wider ones *consist*.[6]

---

[6] [Cf. *A Pluralistic Universe*, Lect. IV, "Concerning Fechner," and Lect. V, "The Compounding of Consciousness."]

V

THE PLACE OF AFFECTIONAL FACTS IN A WORLD OF PURE EXPERIENCE[1]

Common sense and popular philosophy are as dualistic as it is possible to be. Thoughts, we all naturally think, are made of one kind of substance, and things of another. Consciousness, flowing inside of us in the forms of conception or judgment, or concentrating itself in the shape of passion or emotion, can be directly felt as the spiritual activity which it is, and known in contrast with the space-filling, objective "content" which it envelops and accompanies. In opposition to this dualistic philosophy, I tried, in [the first essay] to show that thoughts and things are absolutely homogeneous as to their material, and that their opposition is only one of relation and of function. There is no thought-stuff different from thing-stuff, I said; but the same identical piece of "pure experience" (which was the name I gave to the *materia prima* of everything) can stand alternately for a "fact of consciousness" or for a physical reality, according as it is taken in one context or in another. For the right understanding of what follows, I shall have to presuppose that the reader will have read that [essay].[2]

The commonest objection which the doctrine there laid down runs up against is drawn from the existence of our "affections." In our pleasures and pains, our loves and fears and angers, in

---

[1] [Reprinted from *The Journal of Philosophy, Psychology and Scientific Methods,* vol. II, No. 11, May 25, 1905.]

[2] It will be still better if he shall have also read the [essay] entitled "A World of Pure Experience," which follows [the first] and develops its ideas still farther.

the beauty, comicality, importance or preciousness of certain objects and situations, we have, I am told by many critics, a great realm of experience intuitively recognized as spiritual, made, and felt to be made, of consciousness exclusively, and different in nature from the space-filling kind of being which is enjoyed by physical objects. In Section VII of [the first essay], I treated of this class of experiences very inadequately, because I had to be so brief. I now return to the subject, because I believe that, so far from invalidating my general thesis, these phenomena, when properly analyzed, afford it powerful support.

The central point of the pure-experience theory is that "outer" and "inner" are names for two groups into which we sort experiences according to the way in which they act upon their neighbors. Any one "content," such as *hard,* let us say, can be assigned to either group. In the outer group it is "strong," it acts "energetically" and aggressively. Here whatever is hard interferes with the space its neighbors occupy. It dents them; is impenetrable by them; and we call the hardness then a physical hardness. In the mind, on the contrary, the hard thing is nowhere in particular, it dents nothing, it suffuses through its mental neighbors, as it were, and interpenetrates them. Taken in this group we call both it and them "ideas" or "sensations"; and the basis of the two groups respectively is the different type of interrelation, the mutual impenetrability, on the one hand, and the lack of physical interference and interaction, on the other.

That what in itself is one and the same entity should be able to function thus differently in different contexts is a natural consequence of the extremely complex reticulations in which our experiences come. To her offspring a tigress is tender, but cruel to every other living thing—both cruel and tender, therefore, at once. A mass in movement resists every force that operates contrariwise to its own direction, but to forces that pursue the same direction, or come in at right angles, it is absolutely inert. It is thus both energetic and inert; and the same is true (if you vary the associates properly) of every other piece of experience. It is only towards certain specific groups of associates that the physical energies, as we call them, of a content are put forth. In another group it may be quite inert.

It is possible to imagine a universe of experiences in which the only alternative between neighbors would be either physical interaction or complete inertness. In such a world the mental or the physical *status* of any piece of experience would be unequivocal. When active, it would figure in the physical, and when inactive, in the mental group.

But the universe we live in is more chaotic than this, and there is room in it for the hybrid or ambiguous group of our affectional experiences, of our emotions and appreciative perceptions. In the paragraphs that follow I shall try to show:

(1) That the popular notion that these experiences are intuitively given as purely inner facts is hasty and erroneous; and

(2) That their ambiguity illustrates beautifully my central thesis that subjectivity and objectivity are affairs not of what an experience is aboriginally made of, but of its classification. Classifications depend on our temporary purposes. For certain purposes it is convenient to take things in one set of relations, for other purposes in another set. In the two cases their contexts are apt to be different. In the case of our affectional experiences we have no permanent and steadfast purpose that obliges us to be consistent, so we find it easy to let them float ambiguously, sometimes classing them with our feelings, sometimes with more physical realities, according to caprice or to the convenience of the moment. Thus would these experiences, so far from being an obstacle to the pure experience philosophy, serve as an excellent corroboration of its truth.

First of all, then, it is a mistake to say, with the objectors whom I began by citing, that anger, love and fear are affections purely of the mind. That, to a great extent at any rate, they are simultaneously affections of the body is proved by the whole literature of the James-Lange theory of emotion.[3]

---

[3] [Cf. *The Principles of Psychology*, vol. II, ch. XXV; and "The Physical Basis of Emotion," *The Psychological Review*, vol. I, 1894, p. 516.]

All our pains, moreover, are local, and we are always free to speak of them in objective as well as in subjective terms. We can say that we are aware of a painful place, filling a certain bigness in our organism, or we can say that we are inwardly in a "state" of pain. All our adjectives of worth are similarly ambiguous—I instanced some of the ambiguities [in the first essay].[4] Is the preciousness of a diamond a quality of the gem? or is it a feeling in our mind? Practically we treat it as both or as either, according to the temporary direction of our thought. "Beauty," says Professor Santayana, "is pleasure objectified"; and in Sections 10 and 11 of his work, *The Sense of Beauty,* he treats in a masterly way of this equivocal realm. The various pleasures we receive from an object may count as "feelings" when we take them singly, but when they combine in a total richness, we call the result the "beauty" of the object, and treat it as an outer attribute which our mind perceives. We discover beauty just as we discover the physical properties of things. Training is needed to make us expert in either line. Single sensations also may be ambiguous. Shall we say an "agreeable degree of heat," or an "agreeable feeling" occasioned by the degree of heat? Either will do; and language would lose most of its esthetic and rhetorical value were we forbidden to project words primarily connoting our affections upon the objects by which the affections are aroused. The man is really hateful; the action really mean; the situation really tragic—all in themselves and quite apart from our opinion. We even go so far as to talk of a weary road, a giddy height, a jocund morning or a sullen sky; and the term "indefinite" while usually applied only to our apprehensions, functions as a fundamental physical qualification of things in Spencer's "law of evolution," and doubtless passes with most readers for all right.

Psychologists, studying our perceptions of movement, have unearthed experiences in which movement is felt in general but not ascribed correctly to the body that really

---

[4] [See above, "Does 'Consciousness' Exist?", §VII.]

moves. Thus in optical vertigo, caused by unconscious movements of our eyes, both we and the external universe appear to be in a whirl. When clouds float by the moon, it is as if both clouds and moon and we ourselves shared in the motion. In the extraordinary case of amnesia of the Rev. Mr. Hanna, published by Sidis and Goodhart in their important work on *Multiple Personality,* we read that when the patient first recovered consciousness and "noticed an attendant walk across the room, he identified the movement with that of his own. He did not yet discriminate between his own movements and those outside himself."[5] Such experiences point to a primitive stage of perception in which discriminations afterwards needful have not yet been made. A piece of experience of a determinate sort is there, but there at first as a "pure" fact. Motion originally simply *is;* only later is it confined to this thing or to that. Something like this is true of every experience, however complex, at the moment of its actual presence. Let the reader arrest himself in the act of reading this article now. *Now* this is a pure experience, a phenomenon, or datum, a mere *that* or content of fact. *"Reading" simply is, is there;* and whether there for some one's consciousness, or there for physical nature, is a question not yet put. At the moment, it is there for neither; later we shall probably judge it to have been there for both.

With the affectional experiences which we are considering, the relatively "pure" condition lasts. In practical life no urgent need has yet arisen for deciding whether to treat them as rigorously mental or as rigorously physical facts. So they remain equivocal; and, as the world goes, their equivocality is one of their great conveniences.

The shifting place of "secondary qualities" in the history of philosophy is another excellent proof of the fact that "inner" and "outer" are not coefficients with which experiences come to us aboriginally stamped, but are rather results of a later classification performed by us for particu-

---

[5] Page 102.

lar needs. The common-sense stage of thought is a perfectly definite practical halting-place, the place where we ourselves can proceed to act unhesitatingly. On this stage of thought things act on each other as well as on us by means of their secondary qualities. Sound, as such, goes through the air and can be intercepted. The heat of the fire passes over, as such, into the water which it sets a-boiling. It is the very light of the arc-lamp which displaces the darkness of the midnight street, etc. By engendering and translocating just these qualities, actively efficacious as they seem to be, we ourselves succeed in altering nature so as to suit us; and until more purely intellectual, as distinguished from practical, needs had arisen, no one ever thought of calling these qualities subjective. When, however, Galileo, Descartes, and others found it best for philosophic purposes to class sound, heat, and light along with pain and pleasure as purely mental phenomena, they could do so with impunity.[6]

Even the primary qualities are undergoing the same fate. Hardness and softness are effects on us of atomic interactions, and the atoms themselves are neither hard nor soft, nor solid nor liquid. Size and shape are deemed subjective by Kantians; time itself is subjective according to many philosophers; and even the activity and causal efficacy which lingered in physics long after secondary qualities were banished are now treated as illusory projections outwards of phenomena of our own consciousness. There are no activities or effects in nature, for the most intellectual contemporary school of physical speculation. Nature exhibits only *changes,* which habitually coincide with one another so that their habits are describable in simple "laws."

There is no original spirituality or materiality of being, intuitively discerned, then; but only a translocation of experiences from one world to another; a grouping of them with one set or another of associates for definitely practical or intellectual ends.

I will say nothing here of the persistent ambiguity of *rela-*

---

[6] [Cf. Descartes: *Meditation* II; *Principles of Philosophy,* part I, XLVIII.]

tions. They are undeniable parts of pure experience; yet, while common sense and what I call radical empiricism stand for their being objective, both rationalism and the usual empiricism claim that they are exclusively the "work of the mind"—the finite mind or the absolute mind, as the case may be.

Turn now to those affective phenomena which more directly concern us.

We soon learn to separate the ways in which things appeal to our interests and emotions from the ways in which they act upon one another. It does not *work* to assume that physical objects are going to act outwardly by their sympathetic or antipathetic qualities. The beauty of a thing or its value is no force that can be plotted in a polygon of compositions, nor does its "use" or "significance" affect in the minutest degree its vicissitudes or destiny at the hands of physical nature. Chemical "affinities" are a purely verbal metaphor; and, as I just said, even such things as forces, tensions, and activities can at a pinch be regarded as anthropomorphic projections. So far, then, as the physical world means the collection of contents that determine in each other certain regular changes, the whole collection of our appreciative attributes has to be treated as falling outside of it. If we mean by physical nature whatever lies beyond the surface of our bodies, these attributes are inert throughout the whole extent of physical nature.

Why then do men leave them as ambiguous as they do, and not class them decisively as purely spiritual?

The reason would seem to be that, although they are inert as regards the rest of physical nature, they are not inert as regards that part of physical nature which our own skin covers. It is those very appreciative attributes of things, their dangerousness, beauty, rarity, utility, etc., that primarily appeal to our attention. In our commerce with nature these attributes are what give *emphasis* to objects; and for an object to be emphatic, whatever spiritual fact it may mean, means also that it produces immediate bodily effects upon us, alterations of tone and tension, of heart-beat and breathing, of vascular and visceral action. The "interesting" aspects of things are thus not wholly inert physically, though they be active only in these small corners of physical nature which our bodies occupy. That, however, is enough to save them from being classed as absolutely non-objective.

The attempt, if any one should make it, to sort experience into two absolutely discrete groups, with nothing but inertness in one of them and nothing but activities in the other, would thus receive one check. It would receive another as soon as we examined the more distinctively mental group; for though in that group it be true that things do not act on one another by their physical properties, do not dent each other or set fire to each other, they yet act on each other in the most energetic way by those very characters which are so inert extracorporeally. It is by the interest and importance that experiences have for us, by the emotions they excite, and the purposes they subserve, by their affective values, in short, that their consecution in our several conscious streams, as "thoughts" of ours, is mainly ruled. Desire introduces them; interest holds them; fitness fixes their order and connection. I need only refer for this aspect of our mental life, to Wundt's article "Ueber psychische Causalität," which begins Volume X of his *Philosophische Studien.*[7]

It thus appears that the ambiguous or amphibious *status* which we find our epithets of value occupying is the most natural thing in the world. It would, however, be an unnatural status if the popular opinion which I cited at the outset were correct. If "physical" and "mental" meant two different kinds of intrinsic nature, immediately, intuitively, and infallibly discernible, and each fixed forever in whatever bit of experience it qualified, one does not see how

---

[7] It is enough for my present purpose if the appreciative characters but *seem* to act thus. Believers in an activity *an sich,* other than our mental experiences of activity, will find some farther reflections on the subject in my address on "The Experience of Activity." [The next essay.]

there could ever have arisen any room for doubt or ambiguity. But if, on the contrary, these words are words of sorting, ambiguity is natural. For then, as soon as the relations of a thing are sufficiently various it can be sorted variously. Take a mass of carrion, for example, and the "disgustingness" which for us is a part of the experience. The sun caresses it, and the zephyr woos it as if it were a bed of roses. So the disgustingness fails to *operate* within the realm of suns and breezes,—it does not function as a physical quality. But the carrion "turns our stomach" by what seems a direct operation—it *does* function physically, therefore, in that limited part of physics. We can treat it as physical or as non-physical according as we take it in the narrower or in the wider context, and conversely, of course, we must treat it as non-mental or as mental.

Our body itself is the palmary instance of the ambiguous. Sometimes I treat my body purely as a part of outer nature. Sometimes, again, I think of it as "mine," I sort it with the "me," and then certain local changes and determinations in it pass for spiritual happenings. Its breathing is my "thinking," its sensorial adjustments are my "attention," its kinesthetic alterations are my "efforts," its visceral perturbations are my "emotions." The obstinate controversies that have arisen over such statements as these (which sound so paradoxical, and which can yet be made so seriously) prove how hard it is to decide by bare introspection what it is in experiences that shall make them either spiritual or material. It surely can be nothing intrinsic in the individual experience. It is their way of behaving towards each other, their system of relations, their function; and all these things vary with the context in which we find it opportune to consider them.

I think I may conclude, then (and I hope that my readers are now ready to conclude with me), that the pretended spirituality of our emotions and of our attributes of value, so far from proving an objection to the philosophy of pure experience, does, when rightly discussed and accounted for, serve as one of its best corroborations.

VI

THE EXPERIENCE OF ACTIVITY[1]

BRETHREN OF THE PSYCHOLOGICAL ASSOCIATION:

In casting about me for a subject for your President this year to talk about it has seemed to me that our experiences of activity would form a good one; not only because the topic is so naturally interesting, and because it has lately led to a good deal of rather inconclusive discussion, but because I myself am growing more and more interested in a certain systematic way of handling questions, and want to get others interested also, and this question strikes me as one in which, although I am painfully aware of my inability to communicate new discoveries or to reach definitive conclusions, I yet can show, in a rather definite manner, how the method works.

The way of handling things I speak of, is, as you already will have suspected, that known sometimes as the pragmatic method, sometimes as humanism, sometimes as Deweyism, and in France, by some of the disciples of Bergson, as the Philosophie nouvelle. Professor Woodbridge's *Journal of Philosophy*[2] seems unintentionally to have become a sort of meeting place for those who follow these tendencies in America. There is only a dim identity among them; and the most that can be said at present is that some sort of gestation seems to be in the atmosphere,

---

[1] President's Address before the American Psychological Association, Philadelphia Meeting, December, 1904. [Reprinted from *The Psychological Review,* vol. XII, No. 1, Jan., 1905. The author's corrections have been adopted for the present text. ED.]

[2] [*The Journal of Philosophy, Psychology and Scientific Methods.*]

and that almost any day a man with a genius for finding the right word for things may hit upon some unifying and conciliating formula that will make so much vaguely similar aspiration crystallize into more definite form.

I myself have given the name of "radical empiricism" to that version of the tendency in question which I prefer; and I propose, if you will now let me, to illustrate what I mean by radical empiricism, by applying it to activity as an example, hoping at the same time incidentally to leave the general problem of activity in a slightly—I fear very slightly— more manageable shape than before.

Mr. Bradley calls the question of activity a scandal to philosophy, and if one turns to the current literature of the subject—his own writings included—one easily gathers what he means. The opponents cannot even understand one another. Mr. Bradley says to Mr. Ward: "I do not care what your oracle is, and your preposterous psychology may here be gospel if you please; . . . but if the revelation does contain a meaning, I will commit myself to this: either the oracle is so confused that its signification is not discoverable, or, upon the other hand, if it can be pinned down to any definite statement, then that statement will be false."[3] Mr. Ward in turn says of Mr. Bradley: "I cannot even imagine the state of mind to which his description applies. . . . [It] reads like an unintentional travesty of Herbartian psychology by one who has tried to improve upon it without being at the pains to master it."[4] Münsterberg excludes a view opposed to his own by saying that with any one who holds it a *Verständigung* with him is *"grundsätzlich ausgeschlossen"*; and Royce, in a review of Stout,[5] hauls him over the coals at great length for defending "efficacy" in a way which I, for one, never gathered from reading him, and which I have heard Stout himself say was quite foreign to the intention of his text.

---

[3] *Appearance and Reality,* second edition, pp. 116–117.—Obviously written *at* Ward, though Ward's name is not mentioned.

[4] [*Mind,* vol. XII, 1887, pp. 573–574.]

[5] *Mind,* N. S., vol. VI, [1897], p. 379.

In these discussions distinct questions are habitually jumbled and different points of view are talked of *durcheinander.*

(1) There is a psychological question: "Have we perceptions of activity? and if so, what are they like, and when and where do we have them?"

(2) There is a metaphysical question: "Is there a *fact* of activity? and if so, what idea must we frame of it? What is it like? and what does it do, if it does anything?" And finally there is a logical question:

(3) "Whence do we *know* activity? By our own feelings of it solely? or by some other source of information?" Throughout page after page of the literature one knows not which of these questions is before one; and mere description of the surface-show of experience is proffered as if it implicitly answered every one of them. No one of the disputants, moreover, tries to show what pragmatic consequences his own view would carry, or what assignable particular differences in any one's experience it would make if his adversary's were triumphant.

It seems to me that if radical empiricism be good for anything, it ought, with its pragmatic method and its principle of pure experience, to be able to avoid such tangles, or at least to simplify them somewhat. The pragmatic method starts from the postulate that there is no difference of truth that does n't make a difference of fact somewhere; and it seeks to determine the meaning of all differences of opinion by making the discussion hinge as soon as possible upon some practical or particular issue. The principle of pure experience is also a methodological postulate. Nothing shall be admitted as fact, it says, except what can be experienced at some definite time by some experient; and for every feature of fact ever so experienced, a definite place must be found somewhere in the final system of reality. In other words: Everything real must be experienceable somewhere, and every kind of thing experienced must somewhere be real.

Armed with these rules of method let us see what face the problems of activity present to us.

By the principle of pure experience, either the word "activity" must have no meaning at all, or else the original type and model of what it means must lie in some concrete kind of experience that can be definitely pointed out. Whatever ulterior judgments we may eventually come to make regarding activity, *that sort* of thing will be what the judgments are about. The first step to take, then, is to ask where in the stream of experience we seem to find what we speak of as activity. What we are to think of the activity thus found will be a later question.

Now it is obvious that we are tempted to affirm activity wherever we find anything *going on.* Taken in the broadest sense, any apprehension of something *doing,* is an experience of activity. Were our world describable only by the words "nothing happening," "nothing changing," "nothing doing," we should unquestionably call it an "inactive" world. Bare activity then, as we may call it, means the bare fact of event or change. "Change taking place" is a unique content of experience, one of those "conjunctive" objects which radical empiricism seeks so earnestly to rehabilitate and preserve. The sense of activity is thus in the broadest and vaguest way synonymous with the sense of "life." We should feel our own subjective life at least, even in noticing and proclaiming an otherwise inactive world. Our own reaction on its monotony would be the one thing experienced there in the form of something coming to pass.

This seems to be what certain writers have in mind when they insist that for an experient to be at all is to be active. It seems to justify, or at any rate to explain, Mr. Ward's expression that we *are* only as we are active,[6] for we *are* only as experients; and it rules out Mr. Bradley's contention that "there is no original experience of anything like activ-

---

[6] *Naturalism and Agnosticism,* vol. II, p. 245. One thinks naturally of the peripatetic *actus primus* and *actus secundus* here. ["Actus autem est *duplex: primus* et *secundus.* Actus quidem primus est forma, et integritas sei. Actus autem secundus est operatio." Thomas Aquinas: *Summa Theologica,* edition of Leo XIII, (1894), vol. I, p. 391. Cf. also Blanc: *Dictionnaire de Philosophie,* under "acte." ED.]

ity."[7] What we ought to say about activities thus elementary, whose they are, what they effect, or whether indeed they effect anything at all—these are later questions, to be answered only when the field of experience is enlarged.

Bare activity would thus be predicable, though there were no definite direction, no actor, and no aim. Mere restless zigzag movement, or a wild *Ideenflucht*, or *Rhapsodie der Wahrnehmungen*, as Kant would say,[8] would constitute an active as distinguished from an inactive world.

But in this actual world of ours, as it is given, a part at least of the activity comes with definite direction; it comes with desire and a sense of goal; it comes complicated with resistances which it overcomes or succumbs to, and with the efforts which the feeling of resistance so often provokes; and it is in complex experiences like these that the notions of distinct agents, and of passivity as opposed to activity arise. Here also the notion of causal efficacy comes to birth. Perhaps the most elaborate work ever done in descriptive psychology has been the analysis by various recent writers of the more complex activity-situations.[9] In their descriptions, exquisitely subtle some of them,[10] the activity appears as the *gestaltqualität* or the *fundirte inhalt* (or as whatever else you may please to call the conjunctive form)

---

[7] [*Appearance and Reality,* second edition, p. 116.]

[8] [*Kritik der reinen Vernunft, Werke,* (1905), vol. IV, p. 110 (trans. by Max Müller, second edition, p. 128).]

[9] I refer to such descriptive work as Ladd's (*Psychology, Descriptive and Explanatory,* part I, chap. V, part II, chap. XI, part III, chaps. XXV and XXVI); as Sully's (*The Human Mind,* part V); as Stout's (*Analytic Psychology,* book I, chap. VI, and book II, chaps. I, II, and III); as Bradley's (in his long series of analytic articles on Psychology in *Mind*); as Titchener's (*Outline of Psychology,* part I, chap. VI); as Shand's (*Mind,* N. S., III, 449; IV, 450; VI, 289); as Ward's (*Mind,* XII, 67; 564); as Loveday's (*Mind,* N. S., X, 455); as Lipp's (*Vom Fühlen, Wollen und Denken,* 1902, chaps. II, IV, VI); and as Bergson's (*Revue Philosophique,* LIII, 1)—to mention only a few writings which I immediately recall.

[10] Their existence forms a curious commentary on Prof. Münsterberg's dogma that will-attitudes are not describable. He himself has contributed in a superior way to their description, both in his *Willenshandlung,* and in his *Grundzüge [der Psychologie],* part II, chap. IX, §7.

which the content falls into when we experience it in the ways which the describers set forth. Those factors in those relations are what we mean by activity-situations; and to the possible enumeration and accumulation of their circumstances and ingredients there would seem to be no natural bound. Every hour of human life could contribute to the picture gallery; and this is the only fault that one can find with such descriptive industry—where is it going to stop? Ought we to listen forever to verbal pictures of what we have already in concrete form in our own breasts?[11] They never take us off the superficial plane. We knew the facts already—less spread out and separated, to be sure—but we knew them still. We always felt our own activity, for example, as "the expansion of an idea with which our Self is identified, against an obstacle"; and the following out of such a definition through a multitude of cases elaborates the obvious so as to be little more than an exercise in synonymic speech.

All the descriptions have to trace familiar outlines, and to use familiar terms. The activity is, for example, attributed either to a physical or to a mental agent, and is either aimless or directed. If directed it shows tendency. The tendency may or may not be resisted. If not, we call the activity immanent, as when a body moves in empty space by its momentum, or our thoughts wander at their own sweet will. If resistance is met, *its* agent complicates the situation. If now, in spite of resistance, the original tendency continues, effort makes its appearance, and along with effort, strain or squeeze. Will, in the narrower sense of the word, then comes upon the scene, whenever, along with the tendency, the strain and squeeze are sustained. But the resistance may be great enough to check the tendency, or even to reverse its path. In that case, we (if "we" were the original agents or subjects of the tendency) are overpowered. The phenomenon turns into one of tension simply, or of neces-

---

[11] I ought myself to cry *peccavi,* having been a voluminous sinner in my own chapter on the will. [*Principles of Psychology,* vol. II, chap. XXVI.]

sity succumbed-to, according as the opposing power is only equal, or is superior to ourselves.

Whosoever describes an experience in such terms as these describes an experience *of* activity. If the word have any meaning, it must denote what there is found. *There* is complete activity in its original and first intention. What it is "known-as" is what there appears. The experiencer of such a situation possesses all that the idea contains. He feels the tendency, the obstacle, the will, the strain, the triumph, or the passive giving up, just as he feels the time, the space, the swiftness or intensity, the movement, the weight and color, the pain and pleasure, the complexity, or whatever remaining characters the situation may involve. He goes through all that ever can be imagined where activity is supposed. If we suppose activities to go on outside of our experience, it is in forms like these that we must suppose them, or else give them some other name; for the word "activity" has no imaginable content whatever save these experiences of process, obstruction, striving, strain, or release, ultimate *qualia* as they are of the life given us to be known.

Were this the end of the matter, one might think that whenever we had successfully lived through an activity-situation we should have to be permitted, without provoking contradiction, to say that we had been really active, that we had met real resistance and had really prevailed. Lotze somewhere says that to be an entity all that is necessary is to *gelten* as an entity, to operate, or be felt, experienced, recognized, or in any way realized, as such.[12] In our activity-experiences the activity assuredly fulfills Lotze's demand. It makes itself *gelten*. It is witnessed at its work. No matter what activities there may really be in this extraordinary universe of ours, it is impossible for us to conceive of any one of them being either lived through or authentically known otherwise than in this dramatic shape of something sustaining a felt purpose against felt obstacles and overcoming or being overcome. What "sustaining" means here is clear to

[12] [Cf. above, "A World of Pure Experience," note 9.]

anyone who has lived through the experience, but to no one else; just as "loud," "red," "sweet," mean something only to beings with ears, eyes, and tongues. The *percipi* in these originals of experience is the *esse;* the curtain is the picture. If there is anything hiding in the background, it ought not to be called activity, but should get itself another name.

This seems so obviously true that one might well experience astonishment at finding so many of the ablest writers on the subject flatly denying that the activity we live through in these situations is real. Merely to feel active is not to be active, in their sight. The agents that appear in the experience are not real agents, the resistances do not really resist, the effects that appear are not really effects at all.[13] It is evident from this that mere descriptive analysis

---

[13] *Verborum gratiâ:* "The feeling of activity is not able, *quâ* feeling, to tell us anything about activity" (Loveday: *Mind,* N. S., vol. X, [1901], p. 463); "A sensation or feeling or sense *of* activity . . . is not, looked at in another way, an experience *of* activity at all. It is a mere sensation shut up within which you could by no reflection get the idea of activity. . . . Whether this experience is or is not later on a character essential to our perception and our idea of activity, it, as it comes first, is not in itself an experience of activity at all. It, as it comes first, is only so for extraneous reasons and only so for an outside observer" (Bradley, *Appearance and Reality,* second edition, p. 605); "In dem Tätigkeitsgefühle liegt an sich nicht der geringste Beweis für das Vorhandensein einer psychischen Tätigkeit" (Münsterberg: *Grundzüge der Psychologie*). I could multiply similar quotations and would have introduced some of them into my text to make it more concrete, save that the mingling of different points of view in most of these authors' discussions (not in Münsterberg's) make it impossible to disentangle exactly what they mean. I am sure in any case, to be accused of misrepresenting them totally, even in this note, by omission of the context, so the less I name names and the more I stick to abstract characterization of a merely possible style of opinion, the safer it will be. And apropos of misunderstandings, I may add to this note a complaint on my own account. Professor Stout, in the excellent chapter on "Mental Activity," in vol. I of his *Analytic Psychology,* takes me to task for identifying spiritual activity with certain muscular feelings and gives quotations to bear him out. They are from certain paragraphs on "the Self" in which my attempt was to show what the central nucleus of the activities that we call "ours" is. [*Principles of Psychology,* vol. I, pp. 299–305.] I found it in certain intracephalic movements which we habitually oppose, as "subjective," to the activities of the transcorporeal world. I sought to show that there is no direct evidence that we feel the activity of an inner

of any one of our activity-experiences is not the whole story, that there is something still to tell *about* them that has led such able writers to conceive of a *Simon-pure* activity, an activity *an sich,* that does, and doesn't merely appear to us to do, and compared with whose real doing all this phenomenal activity is but a specious sham.

---

spiritual agent as such (I should now say the activity of "consciousness" as such, see [the first essay], "Does 'Consciousness' Exist?"). There are, in fact, three distinguishable "activities" in the field of discussion: the elementary activity involved in the mere *that* of experience, in the fact that *something* is going on, and the farther specification of this *something* into two *whats,* an activity felt as "ours," and an activity ascribed to objects. Stout, as I apprehend him, identifies "our" activity with that of the total experience-process, and when I circumscribe it as a part thereof, accuses me of treating it as a sort of external appendage to itself (Stout: *op. cit.,* vol. I, pp. 162–163), as if I "separated the activity from the process which is active." But all the processes in question are active, and their activity is inseparable from their being. My book raised only the question of *which* activity deserved the name of "ours." So far as we are "persons," and contrasted and opposed to an "environment," movements in our body figure as our activities; and I am unable to find any other activities that are ours in this strictly personal sense. There is a wider sense in which the whole "choir of heaven and furniture of the earth," and their activities, are ours, for they are our "objects." But "we" are here only another name for the total process of experience, another name for all that is, in fact; and I was dealing with the personal and individualized self exclusively in the passages with which Professor Stout finds fault.

The individualized self, which I believe to be the only thing properly called self, is a part of the content of the world experienced. The world experienced (otherwise called the "field of consciousness") comes at all times with our body at its center, center of vision, center of action, center of interest. Where the body is is "here": when the body acts is "now"; what the body touches is "this"; all other things are "there" and "then" and "that." These words of emphasized position imply a systematization of things with reference to a focus of action and interest which lies in the body; and the systematization is now so instinctive (was it ever not so?) that no developed or active experience exists for us at all except in that ordered form. So far as "thoughts" and "feelings" can be active, their activity terminates in the activity of the body, and only through first arousing its activities can they begin to change those of the rest of the world. The body is the storm center, the origin of co-ordinates, the constant place of stress in all that experience-train. Everything circles round it, and is felt from its point of view. The word "I," then, is primarily a noun of position, just like "this" and "here." Activities attached to "this" position have prerogative emphasis, and, if activities have feelings, must be felt in a peculiar way. The word "my" designates the kind

The metaphysical question opens here; and I think that the state of mind of one possessed by it is often something like this: "It is all very well," we may imagine him saying, "to talk about certain experience-series taking on the form of feelings of activity, just as they might take on musical or geometric forms. Suppose that they do so; suppose we feel a will to stand a strain. Does our feeling do more than *record* the fact that the strain is sustained? The *real* activity, meanwhile, is the *doing* of the fact; and what is the doing made of before the record is made. What in the will *enables* it to act thus? And these trains of experience themselves, in which activities appear, what makes them *go* at all? Does the activity in one bit of experience bring the next bit into being? As an empiricist you cannot say so, for you have just declared activity to be only a kind of synthetic object, or conjunctive relation experienced between bits of experience already made. But what made them at all? What propels experience *überhaupt* into being? *There* is the activity that *operates;* the activity *felt* is only its superficial sign."

To the metaphysical question, popped upon us in this way, I must pay serious attention ere I end my remarks; but, before doing so, let me show that without leaving the immediate reticulations of experience, or asking what makes activity itself act, we still find the distinction between less real and more real activities forced upon us, and are driven to much soul-searching on the purely phenomenal plane.

We must not forget, namely, in talking of the ultimate character of our activity-experiences, that each of them is but a portion of a wider world, one link in the vast chain of processes of experience out of which history is made. Each partial process, to him who lives through it, defines itself by its origin and its goal; but to an observer with a wider mind-span who should live outside of it, that goal would appear

---

of emphasis. I see no inconsistency whatever in defending, on the one hand, "my" activities as unique and opposed to those of outer nature, and, on the other hand, in affirming, after introspection, that they consist in movements in the head. The "my" of them is the emphasis, the feeling of perspective-interest in which they are dyed.

but as a provisional halting-place, and the subjectively felt activity would be seen to continue into objective activities that led far beyond. We thus acquire a habit, in discussing activity-experiences, of defining them by their relation to something more. If an experience be one of narrow span, it will be mistaken as to what activity it is and whose. You think that *you* are acting while you are only obeying someone's push. You think you are doing *this,* but you are doing something of which you do not dream. For instance, you think you are but drinking this glass; but you are really creating the liver-cirrhosis that will end your days. You think you are just driving this bargain, but, as Stevenson says somewhere, you are laying down a link in the policy of mankind.

Generally speaking, the onlooker, with his wider field of vision, regards the *ultimate outcome* of an activity as what it is more really doing; and *the most previous agent* ascertainable, being the first source of action, he regards as the most real agent in the field. The others but transmit the agent's impulse; on him we put responsibility; we name him when one asks us "Who's to blame?"

But the most previous agents ascertainable, instead of being of longer span, are often of much shorter span than the activity in view. Brain-cells are our best example. My brain-cells are believed to excite each other from next to next (by contiguous transmission of katabolic alteration, let us say) and to have been doing so long before this present stretch of lecturing-activity on my part began. If any one cell-group stops its activity, the lecturing will cease or show disorder of form. *Cessante causa, cessat et effectus*—does not this look as if the short-span brain activities were the more real activities, and the lecturing activities on my part only their effects? Moreover, as Hume so clearly pointed out,[14] in my mental activity-situation the words physically to be uttered are represented as the activity's immediate goal.

---

[14] [*Enquiry Concerning Human Understanding,* sect. VII, part I, Selby-Bigge's edition, pp. 65 ff.]

These words, however, cannot be uttered without intermediate physical processes in the bulb and vagi nerves, which processes nevertheless fail to figure in the mental activity-series at all. That series, therefore, since it leaves out vitally real steps of action, cannot represent the real activities. It is something purely subjective; the *facts* of activity are elsewhere. They are something far more interstitial, so to speak, than what my feelings record.

The *real* facts of activity that have in point of fact been systematically pleaded for by philosophers have, so far as my information goes, been of three principal types.

The first type takes a consciousness of wider time-span than ours to be the vehicle of the more real activity. Its will is the agent, and its purpose is the action done.

The second type assumes that "ideas" struggling with one another are the agents, and that the prevalence of one set of them is the action.

The third type believes that nerve-cells are the agents, and that resultant motor discharges are the acts achieved.

Now if we must de-realize our immediately felt activity-situations for the benefit of either of these types of substitute, we ought to know what the substitution practically involves. *What practical difference ought it to make if,* instead of saying naïvely that "I" am active now in delivering this address, I say that *a wider thinker is active,* or that *certain ideas are active,* or that *certain nerve-cells are active,* in producing the result?

This would be the pragmatic meaning of the three hypotheses. Let us take them in succession in seeking a reply.

If we assume a wider thinker, it is evident that his purposes envelop mine. I am really lecturing *for* him; and although I cannot surely know to what end, yet if I take him religiously, I can trust it to be a good end, and willingly connive. I can be happy in thinking that my activity transmits his impulse, and that his ends prolong my own. So long as I take him religiously, in short, he does not de-realize my activities. He tends rather to corroborate the reality of them, so long as I believe both them and him to be good.

When now we turn to ideas, the case is different, inasmuch as ideas are supposed by the association psychology to influence each other only from next to next. The "span" of an idea or pair of ideas, is assumed to be much smaller instead of being larger than that of my total conscious field. The same results may get worked out in both cases, for this address is being given anyhow. But the ideas supposed to "really" work it out had no prevision of the whole of it; and if I was lecturing for an absolute thinker in the former case, so, by similar reasoning, are my ideas now lecturing for me, that is, accomplishing unwittingly a result which I approve and adopt. But, when this passing lecture is over, there is nothing in the bare notion that ideas have been its agents that would seem to guarantee that my present purposes in lecturing will be prolonged. *I* may have ulterior developments in view; but there is no certainty that my ideas as such will wish to, or be able to, work them out.

The like is true if nerve-cells be the agents. The activity of a nerve-cell must be conceived of as a tendency of exceedingly short reach, an "impulse" barely spanning the way to the next cell—for surely that amount of actual "process" must be "experienced" by the cells if what happens between them is to deserve the name of activity at all. But here again the gross resultant, as *I* perceive it, is indifferent to the agents, and neither wished or willed or foreseen. Their being agents now congruous with my will gives me no guarantee that like results will recur again from their activity. In point of fact, all sorts of other results do occur. My mistakes, impotencies, perversions, mental obstructions, and frustrations generally, are also results of the activity of cells. Although these are letting me lecture now, on other occasions they make me do things that I would willingly not do.

The question *Whose is the real activity?* is thus tantamount to the question *What will be the actual results?* Its interest is dramatic; how will things work out? If the agents are of one sort, one way; if of another sort, they may work out very differently. The pragmatic meaning of the various alternatives, in short, is great. It makes no merely verbal difference which opinion we take up.

You see it is the old dispute come back! Materialism and teleology; elementary short-span actions summing themselves "blindly," or far foreseen ideals coming with effort into act.

Naïvely we believe, and humanly and dramatically we like to believe, that activities both of wider and of narrower span are at work in life together, that both are real, and that the long-span tendencies yoke the others in their service, encouraging them in the right direction, and damping them when they tend in other ways. But how to represent clearly the *modus operandi* of such steering of small tendencies by large ones is a problem which metaphysical thinkers will have to ruminate upon for many years to come. Even if such control should eventually grow clearly picturable, the question how far it is successfully exerted in this actual world can be answered only by investigating the details of fact. No philosophic knowledge of the general nature and constitution of tendencies, or of the relation of larger to smaller ones, can help us to predict which of all the various competing tendencies that interest us in this universe are likeliest to prevail. We know as an empirical fact that far-seeing tendencies often carry out their purpose, but we know also that they are often defeated by the failure of some contemptibly small process on which success depends. A little thrombus in a statesman's meningeal artery will throw an empire out of gear. I can therefore not even hint at any solution of the pragmatic issue. I have only wished to show you that that issue is what gives the real interest to all inquiries into what kinds of activity may be real. Are the forces that really act in the world more foreseeing or more blind? As between "our" activities as "we" experience them, and those of our ideas, or of our brain-cells, the issue is well-defined.

I said a while back[15] that I should return to the "meta-

---

[15] Page 90.

physical" question before ending; so, with a few words about that, I will now close my remarks.

In whatever form we hear this question propounded, I think that it always arises from two things, a belief that *causality* must be exerted in activity, and a wonder as to how causality is made. If we take an activity-situation at its face-value, it seems as if we caught *in flagrante delicto* the very power that makes facts come and be. I now am eagerly striving, for example, to get this truth which I seem half to perceive, into words which shall make it show more clearly. If the words come, it will seem as if the striving itself had drawn or pulled them into actuality out from the state of merely possible being in which they were. How is this feat performed? How does the pulling *pull?* How do I get my hold on words not yet existent, and when they come by what means have I *made* them come? Really it is the problem of creation; for in the end the question is: How do I make them *be?* Real activities are those that really make things be, without which the things are not, and with which they are there. Activity, so far as we merely feel it, on the other hand, is only an impression of ours, it may be maintained; and an impression is, for all this way of thinking, only a shadow of another fact.

Arrived at this point, I can do little more than indicate the principles on which, as it seems to me, a radically empirical philosophy is obliged to rely in handling such a dispute.

If there *be* real creative activities in being, radical empiricism must say, somewhere they must be immediately lived. Somewhere the *that* of efficacious causing and the *what* of it must be experienced in one, just as the what and the that of "cold" are experienced in one whenever a man has the sensation of cold here and now. It boots not to say that our sensations are fallible. They are indeed; but to see the thermometer contradict us when we say "it is cold" does not abolish cold as a specific nature from the universe. Cold is in the arctic circle if not here. Even so, to feel that our train is moving when the train beside our window moves, to see

the moon through a telescope come twice as near, or to see
two pictures as one solid when we look through a stereo-
scope at them, leaves motion, nearness, and solidity still in
being—if not here, yet each in its proper seat elsewhere.
And wherever the seat of real causality *is,* as ultimately
known "for true" (in nerve-processes, if you will, that cause
our feelings of activity as well as the movements which
these seem to prompt), a philosophy of pure experience can
consider the real causation as no other *nature* of thing than
that which even in our most erroneous experiences appears
to be at work. Exactly what appears there is what we *mean*
by working, though we may later come to learn that working was not exactly *there.* Sustaining, persevering, striving,
paying with effort as we go, hanging on, and finally achieving our intention—this *is* action, this *is* effectuation in the
only shape in which, by a pure experience-philosophy, the
whereabouts of it anywhere can be discussed. Here is creation in its first intention, here is causality at work.[16] To
treat this offhand as the bare illusory surface of a world
whose real causality is an unimaginable ontological principle hidden in the cubic deeps, is, for the more empirical way
of thinking, only animism in another shape. You explain
your given fact by your "principle," but the principle itself,
when you look clearly at it, turns out to be nothing but a

---

[16] Let me not be told that this contradicts [the first essay], "Does
'Consciousness' Exist?" (see especially page 17), in which it was said
that while "thoughts" and "things" have the same natures, the natures
work "energetically" on each other in the things (fire burns, water wets,
etc.) but not in the thoughts. Mental activity-trains are composed of
thoughts, yet their members do work on each other, they check, sustain,
and introduce. They do so when the activity is merely associational as
well as when effort is there. But, and this is my reply, they do so by
other parts of their nature than those that energize physically. One
thought in every developed activity-series is a desire or thought of purpose, and all the other thoughts acquire a feeling tone from their relation of harmony or oppugnancy to this. The interplay of these secondary
tones (among which "interest," "difficulty," and "effort" figure) runs the
drama in the mental series. In what we term the physical drama these
qualities play absolutely no part. The subject needs careful working
out; but I can see no inconsistency.

previous little spiritual copy of the fact. Away from that one and only kind of fact your mind, considering causality, can never get.[17]

I conclude, then, that real effectual causation as an ultimate nature, as a "category," if you like, of reality, is *just what we feel it to be*, just that kind of conjunction which our own activity-series reveal. We have the whole butt and being of it in our hands; and the healthy thing for philosophy is to leave off grubbing underground for what effects effectuation, or what makes action act, and to try to solve the concrete questions of where effectuation in this world is located, of which things are the true causal agents there, and of what the more remote effects consist.

---

[17] I have found myself more than once accused in print of being the assertor of a metaphysical principle of activity. Since literary misunderstandings retard the settlement of problems, I should like to say that such an interpretation of the pages I have published on Effort and on Will is absolutely foreign to what I meant to express. [*Principles of Psychology,* vol. II, ch. XXVI.] I owe all my doctrines on this subject to Renouvier; and Renouvier, as I understand him, is (or at any rate then was) an out and out phenomenist, a denier of "forces" in the most strenuous sense. [Cf. Ch. Renouvier: *Esquisse d'une Classification Systématique des Doctrines Philosophiques* (1885), vol. II, pp. 390–392; *Essais de Critique Générale* (1859), vol. II, §§ix, xiii. For an acknowledgment of the author's general indebtedness to Renouvier, cf. *Some Problems of Philosophy,* p. 165, note. ED.] Single clauses in my writing, or sentences read out of their connection, may possibly have been compatible with a transphenomenal principle of energy; but I defy anyone to show a single sentence which, taken with its context, should be naturally held to advocate that view. The misinterpretation probably arose at first from my defending (after Renouvier) the indeterminism of our efforts. "Free will" was supposed by my critics to involve a supernatural agent. As a matter of plain history the only "free will" I have ever thought of defending is the character of novelty in fresh activity-situations. If an activity-process is the form of a whole "field of consciousness," and if each field of consciousness is not only in its totality unique (as is now commonly admitted) but has its elements unique (since in that situation they are all dyed in the total) then novelty is perpetually entering the world and what happens there is not pure *repetition,* as the dogma of the literal uniformity of nature requires. Activity-situations come, in short, each with an original touch. A "principle" of free will if there were one, would doubtless manifest itself in such phenomena, but I never say, nor do I now see, what the principle could do except rehearse the phenomenon beforehand, or why it ever should be invoked.

From this point of view the greater sublimity tradition-
ally attributed to the metaphysical inquiry, the grubbing
inquiry, entirely disappears. If we could know what causation really and transcendentally is in itself, the only *use* of
the knowledge would be to help us to recognize an actual
cause when we had one, and so to track the future course of
operations more intelligently out. The mere abstract
inquiry into causation's hidden nature is not more sublime
than any other inquiry equally abstract. Causation inhab-
its no more sublime level than anything else. It lives, apparently, in the dirt of the world as well as in the absolute, or
in man's unconquerable mind. The worth and interest of the
world consists not in its elements, be these elements things,
or be they the conjunctions of things; it exists rather in the
dramatic outcome in the whole process, and in the meaning
of the succession stages which the elements work out.

My colleague and master, Josiah Royce, in a page of his
review of Stout's *Analytic Psychology*[18] has some fine words
on this point with which I cordially agree. I cannot agree
with his separating the notion of efficacy from that of activity altogether (this I understand to be one contention of his)
for activities are efficacious whenever they are real activities at all. But the inner nature both of efficacy and of activity are superficial problems, I understand Royce to say; and
the only point for us in solving them would be their possible
use in helping us to solve the far deeper problem of the
course and meaning of the world of life. Life, says our colleague, is full of significance, of meaning, of success and of
defeat, of hoping and of striving, of longing, of desire, and of
inner value. It is a total presence that embodies worth. To
live our own lives better in this presence is the true reason
why we wish to know the elements of things; so even we
psychologists must end on this pragmatic note.

The urgent problems of activity are thus more concrete.
They are all problems of the true relation of longer-span to
shorter-span activities. When, for example, a number of

---

[18] *Mind*, N. S., vol. VI, 1897; cf. pp. 392–393.

"ideas" (to use the name traditional in psychology) grow confluent in a larger field of consciousness, do the smaller activities still co-exist with the wider activities then experienced by the conscious subject? And, if so, do the wide activities accompany the narrow ones inertly, or do they exert control? Or do they perhaps utterly supplant and replace them and short-circuit their effects? Again, when a mental activity-process and a brain-cell series of activities both terminate in the same muscular movement, does the mental process steer the neural processes or not? Or, on the other hand, does it independently short-circuit their effects? Such are the questions that we must begin with. But so far am I from suggesting any definitive answer to such questions, that I hardly yet can put them clearly. They lead, however, into that region of panpsychic and ontologic speculation of which Professors Bergson and Strong have lately enlarged the literature in so able and interesting a way.[19] The results of these authors seem in many respects dissimilar, and I understand them as yet but imperfectly; but I cannot help suspecting that the direction of their work is very promising, and that they have the hunter's instinct for the fruitful trails.

---

[19] [Cf. *A Pluralistic Universe*, Lect. VI (on Bergson); H. Bergson: *Creative Evolution*, trans. by A. Mitchell; C. A. Strong: *Why the Mind Has a Body*, ch. XII. ED.]

VII
THE ESSENCE OF HUMANISM[1]

Humanism is a ferment that has "come to stay."[2] It is not a single hypothesis or theorem, and it dwells on no new facts. It is rather a slow shifting in the philosophic perspective, making things appear as from a new center of interest or point of sight. Some writers are strongly conscious of the shifting, others half unconscious, even though their own vision may have undergone much change. The result is no small confusion in debate, the half-conscious humanists often taking part against the radical ones, as if they wished to count upon the other side.[3]

If humanism really be the name for such a shifting of perspective, it is obvious that the whole scene of the philosophic stage will change in some degree if humanism prevails. The emphasis of things, their foreground and background distribution, their sizes and values, will not keep

---

[1] [Reprinted from *The Journal of Philosophy, Psychology and Scientific Methods,* vol. II, No. 5, March 2, 1905. Also reprinted, with slight changes in *The Meaning of Truth,* pp. 121–135. The author's corrections have been adopted for the present text. ED.]

[2] [Written *apropos* of the appearance of three articles in *Mind,* N. S., vol. XIV, No. 53, January, 1905: "'Absolute' and 'Relative' Truth," H. H. Joachim; "Professor James on 'Humanism and Truth,'" H. W. B. Joseph; "Applied Axioms," A. Sidgwick. Of these articles the second and third "continue the humanistic (or pragmatistic) controversy," the first "deeply connects with it." ED.]

[3] Professor Baldwin, for example. His address "On Selective Thinking" (*Psychological Review,* [vol. V], 1898, reprinted in his volume, *Development and Evolution*) seems to me an unusually well-written pragmatic manifesto. Nevertheless in "The Limits of Pragmatism" (*ibid.,* [vol. XI], 1904), he (much less clearly) joins in the attack.

just the same.[4] If such pervasive consequences be involved in humanism, it is clear that no pains which philosophers may take, first in defining it, and then in furthering, checking, or steering its progress, will be thrown away.

It suffers badly at present from incomplete definition. Its most systematic advocates, Schiller and Dewey, have published fragmentary programs only; and its bearing on many vital philosophic problems has not been traced except by adversaries who, scenting heresies in advance, have showered blows on doctrines—subjectivism and scepticism, for example—that no good humanist finds it necessary to entertain. By their still greater reticences, the anti-humanists have, in turn, perplexed the humanists. Much of the controversy has involved the word "truth." It is always good in debate to know your adversary's point of view authentically. But the critics of humanism never define exactly what the word "truth" signifies when they use it themselves. The humanists have to guess at their view; and the result has doubtless been much beating of the air. Add to all this, great individual differences in both camps, and it becomes clear that nothing is so urgently needed, at the stage which things have reached at present, as a sharper definition by each side of its central point of view.

Whoever will contribute any touch of sharpness will help us to make sure of what's what and who is who. Anyone can contribute such a definition, and, without it, no one knows exactly where he stands. If I offer my own provisional defi-

---

[4] The ethical changes, it seems to me, are beautifully made evident in Professor Dewey's series of articles, which will never get the attention they deserve till they are printed in a book. I mean: "The Significance of Emotions," *Psychological Review,* vol. II, [1895], p. 13; "The Reflex Arc Concept in Psychology," *ibid.,* vol. III [1896], p. 357; "Psychology and Social Practice," *ibid.,* vol. VII, [1900], p. 105; "Interpretation of Savage Mind," *ibid.,* vol. IX, [1902], p. 217; "Green's Theory of the Moral Motive," *Philosophical Review,* vol. I, [1892], p. 593; "Self-realization as the Moral Ideal," *ibid.,* vol. II, [1893], p. 652; "The Psychology of Effort," *ibid.,* vol. VI, [1897], p. 43; "The Evolutionary Method as Applied to Morality," *ibid.,* vol. XI, [1902], pp. 107, 353; "Evolution and Ethics," *Monist,* vol. VIII, [1898], p. 321; to mention only a few.

nition of humanism[5] now and here, others may improve it, some adversary may be led to define his own creed more sharply by the contrast, and a certain quickening of the crystallization of general opinion may result.

I

The essential service of humanism, as I conceive the situation, is to have seen that *though one part of our experience may lean upon another part to make it what it is in any one of several aspects in which it may be considered, experience as a whole is self-containing and leans on nothing.*

Since this formula also expresses the main contention of transcendental idealism, it needs abundant explication to make it unambiguous. It seems, at first sight, to confine itself to denying theism and pantheism. But, in fact, it need not deny either; everything would depend on the exegesis; and if the formula ever became canonical, it would certainly develop both right-wing and left-wing interpreters. I myself read humanism theistically and pluralistically. If there be a God, he is no absolute all-experiencer, but simply the experiencer of widest actual conscious span. Read thus, humanism is for me a religion susceptible of reasoned defense, though I am well aware how many minds there are to whom it can appeal religiously only when it has been monistically translated. Ethically the pluralistic form of it takes for me a stronger hold on reality than any other philosophy I know of—it being essentially a *social* philosophy, a philosophy of *"co,"* in which conjunctions do the work. But my primary reason for advocating it is its matchless intellectual economy. It gets rid, not only of the standing "problems" that monism engenders ("problem of evil," "problem of freedom," and the like), but of other metaphysical mysteries and paradoxes as well.

It gets rid, for example, of the whole agnostic controversy,

---

[5] [The author employs the term "humanism" either as a synonym for "radical empiricism"; or as that general philosophy of life of which "radical empiricism" is the theoretical ground (cf. §1 below). For other discussions of "humanism," cf. below, essay XI, and *The Meaning of Truth*, essay III. Ed.]

by refusing to entertain the hypothesis of trans-empirical reality at all. It gets rid of any need for an absolute of the Bradleyan type (avowedly sterile for intellectual purposes) by insisting that the conjunctive relations found within experience are faultlessly real. It gets rid of the need of an absolute of the Roycean type (similarly sterile) by its pragmatic treatment of the problem of knowledge [a treatment of which I have already given a version in two very inadequate articles].[6] As the views of knowledge, reality and truth imputed to humanism have been those so far most fiercely attacked, it is in regard to these ideas that a sharpening of focus seems most urgently required. I proceed therefore to bring the view which *I* impute to humanism in these respects into focus as briefly as I can.

II

If the central humanistic thesis, printed above in italics, be accepted, it will follow that, if there be any such thing at all as knowing, the knower and the object known must both be portions of experience. One part of experience must, therefore, either

(1) Know another part of experience—in other words, parts must, as Professor Woodbridge says,[7] represent *one another* instead of representing realities outside of "consciousness"— this case is that of conceptual knowledge; or else

(2) They must simply exist as so many ultimate *thats* or facts of being, in the first instance; and then, as a secondary complication, and without doubling up its entitative singleness, any one and the same *that* must figure alternately as a thing known and as a knowledge of the thing, by reason of two divergent kinds of context into which, in the general course of experience, it gets woven.[8]

---

[6] [The articles referred to are "Does 'Consciousness' Exist?" and "A World of Pure Experience," reprinted above.]

[7] In *Science,* November 4, 1904, p. 599.

[8] This statement is probably excessively obscure to any one who has not read my two articles, "Does 'Consciousness' Exist?" and "A World of Pure Experience."

This second case is that of sense-perception. There is a stage of thought that goes beyond common sense, and of it I shall say more presently; but the common-sense stage is a perfectly definite halting-place of thought, primarily for purposes of action; and, so long as we remain on the common-sense stage of thought, object and subject *fuse* in the fact of "presentation" or sense-perception—the pen and hand which I now *see* writing, for example, *are* the physical realities which those words designate. In this case there is no self-transcendency implied in the knowing. Humanism, here, is only a more comminuted *Identitätsphilosophie*.[9]

In case (1), on the contrary, the representative experience does transcend itself in knowing the other experience that is its object. No one can talk of the knowledge of the one by the other without seeing them as numerically distinct entities, of which the one lies beyond the other and away from it, along some direction and with some interval, that can be definitely named. But, if the talker be a humanist, he must also see this distance-interval concretely and pragmatically, and confess it to consist of other intervening experiences—of possible ones, at all events, if not of actual. To call my present idea of my dog, for example, cognitive of the real dog means that, as the actual tissue of experience is constituted, the idea is capable of leading into a chain of other experiences on my part that go from next to next and terminate at last in vivid sense-perceptions of a jumping, barking, hairy body. Those *are* the real dog, the dog's full presence, for my common sense. If the supposed talker is a profound philosopher, although they may not *be* the real dog for him, they *mean* the real dog, are practical substitutes for the real dog, as the representation was a practical substitute for them, that real dog being a lot of atoms, say, or of mind-stuff, that lie *where* the sense-perceptions lie in his experience as well as in my own.

---

[9] [Cf. essay IV above, "How Two Minds Can Know One Thing," §IV.]

III

The philosopher here stands for the stage of thought that goes beyond the stage of common sense; and the difference is simply that he "interpolates" and "extrapolates," where common sense does not. For common sense, two men see the same identical real dog. Philosophy, noting actual differences in their perceptions, points out the duality of these latter, and interpolates something between them as a more real terminus—first, organs, viscera, etc.; next, cells; then, ultimate atoms; lastly, mind-stuff perhaps. The original sense-termini of the two men, instead of coalescing with each other and with the real dog-object, as at first supposed, are thus held by philosophers to be separated by invisible realities with which, at most, they are conterminous.

Abolish, now, one of the percipients, and the interpolation changes into "extrapolation." The sense-terminus of the remaining percipient is regarded by the philosopher as not quite reaching reality. He has only carried the procession of experiences, the philosopher thinks, to a definite, because practical, halting-place somewhere on the way towards an absolute truth that lies beyond.

The humanist sees all the time, however, that there is no absolute transcendency even about the more absolute realities thus conjectured or believed in. The viscera and cells are only possible percepts following upon that of the outer body. The atoms again, though we may never attain to human means of perceiving them, are still defined perceptually. The mind-stuff itself is conceived as a kind of experience; and it is possible to frame the hypothesis (such hypotheses can by no logic be excluded from philosophy) of two knowers of a piece of mind-stuff and the mind-stuff itself becoming "confluent" at the moment at which our imperfect knowing might pass into knowing of a completed type. Even so do you and I habitually represent our two perceptions and the real dog as confluent, though only provisionally, and for the common-sense stage of thought. If my pen be inwardly made of mind-stuff, there is no confluence *now* between that mind-stuff and my visual perception of the pen. But conceivably there might come to be such confluence; for, in the case of my hand, the visual sensations and the inward feelings of the hand, its mind-stuff, so to speak, are even now as confluent as any two things can be.

There is, thus, no breach in humanistic epistemology. Whether knowledge be taken as ideally perfected, or only as true enough to pass muster for practice, it is hung on one continuous scheme. Reality, howsoever remote, is always defined as a terminus within the general possibilities of experience; and what knows it is defined as an experience *that "represents" it, in the sense of being substitutable for it in our thinking* because it leads to the same associates, *or in the sense of "pointing to it"* through a chain of other experiences that either intervene or may intervene.

Absolute reality here bears the same relation to sensation as sensation bears to conception or imagination. Both are provisional or final termini, sensation being only the terminus at which the practical man habitually stops, while the philosopher projects a "beyond" in the shape of more absolute reality. These termini, for the practical and the philosophical stages of thought respectively, are self-supporting. They are not "true" of anything else, they simply *are,* are *real.* They "lean on nothing," as my italicized formula said. Rather does the whole fabric of experience lean on them, just as the whole fabric of the solar system, including many relative positions, leans, for its absolute position in space, on any one of its constituent stars. Here, again, one gets a new *Identitätsphilosophie* in pluralistic form.[10]

IV

If I have succeeded in making this at all clear (though I fear that brevity and abstractness between them may have made me fail), the reader will see that the "truth" of our mental operations must always be an intra-experiential affair. A conception is reckoned true by common sense when

---

[10] [Cf. essay IV above, "How Two Minds Can Know One Thing," §IV.]

it can be made to lead to a sensation. The sensation, which for common sense is not so much "true" as "real," is held to be *provisionally* true by the philosopher just in so far as it *covers* (abuts at, or occupies the place of) a still more absolutely real experience, in the possibility of which to some remoter experient the philosopher finds reason to believe.

Meanwhile what actually *does* count for true to any individual trower, whether he be philosopher or common man, is always a result of his *apperceptions*. If a novel experience, conceptual or sensible, contradict too emphatically our pre-existent system of beliefs, in ninety-nine cases out of a hundred it is treated as false. Only when the older and the newer experiences are congruous enough to mutually apperceive and modify each other, does what we treat as an advance in truth result. [Having written of this point in an article in reply to Mr. Joseph's criticism of my humanism, I will say no more about truth here, but refer the reader to that review.[11]] In no case, however, need truth consist in a relation between our experiences and something archetypal or trans-experiential. Should we ever reach absolutely terminal experiences, experiences in which we all agreed, which were superseded by no revised continuations, these would not be *true,* they would be *real,* they would simply *be,* and be indeed the angles, corners, and linchpins of all reality, on which the truth of everything else would be stayed. Only such *other* things as led to these by satisfactory conjunctions would be "true." Satisfactory connection of some sort with such termini is all that the word "truth" means. On the common-sense stage of thought sense-presentations serve as such termini. Our ideas and concepts and scientific theories pass for true only so far as they harmoniously lead back to the world of sense.

I hope that many humanists will endorse this attempt of mine to trace the more essential features of that way of

---

[11] [The review referred to is reprinted as essay XI below, under the title "Humanism and Truth Once More." ED.]

viewing things. I feel almost certain that Messrs. Dewey and Schiller will do so. If the attackers will also take some slight account of it, it may be that discussion will be a little less wide of the mark than it has hitherto been.

VIII
The Notion of Consciousness[1]

[Translator's note: A conscious effort has been made to use the English terminology of the preceding articles. At times a choice was available between pairs of apparent synonyms, such as "unextended" and "inextensive." Of the pair "mental" and "psychic," the latter term was avoided here because of its recent connotation "occult, supernatural." "Solvent" has replaced James's "menstruum" because of that term's comparative rarity.]

I would like to communicate to you certain doubts that have occurred to me regarding the notion of consciousness which is prevalent in all our treatises on psychology.

Psychology is usually defined as the science of the facts of consciousness, or of the "phenomena" or also the "states" of consciousness. Whether it is acknowledged to be associated with personal egos, or it is believed to be impersonal like Kant's "transcendental ego" or the *Bewusstheit* or *Bewusstsein überhaupt* of our contemporaries in Germany, this consciousness is always regarded as possessing an essence of its own, absolutely distinct from the essence of material things, which it has the mysterious power to represent and to know. Material facts, taken in their materiality, are not *felt*, are not *objects of experience*, do not *get reported*. In order for them to take the form of the system in

---

[1] [A communication made (in French) at the Fifth International Congress of Psychology, in Rome, April 30, 1905. It is reprinted from the *Archives de Psychologie*, vol. V, No. 17, June, 1905.] This communication is the summary, necessarily very condensed, of views which the author presented during the last few months in a series of articles published in the *Journal of Philosophy, Psychology and Scientific Methods*, 1904 and 1905. [The series of articles referred to is reprinted above. Ed.]

which we feel ourselves to be living, they must *appear*, and this fact of appearing, added to their raw existence, is called the consciousness that we have of them, or, perhaps, according to the panpsychist hypothesis, the consciousness that they have of themselves.

This is the inveterate dualism that is seemingly impossible to eliminate from our view of the world. This world may very well exist in itself, but we know nothing of this, because for us it is exclusively an object of experience; and the indispensable condition for this purpose is that it be reported to witnesses, that it be known by a subject or subjects through their mind. Object and subject: those are the two legs without which it seems that philosophy cannot take one step forward.

All the schools are in agreement in that regard, Scholasticism, Cartesianism, Kantism, Neo-Kantism: they all acknowledge this fundamental duality. The positivism or agnosticism of our days, which boasts of its dependence on the natural sciences, likes to adopt the name of monism, it's true. But it is merely a verbal monism. It posits an unknown reality, but it tells us that this reality always presents itself in two "aspects," consciousness on one side and matter on the other, and those two sides remain just as irreducible as the fundamental attributes of Spinoza's God, extension and thought. At bottom, contemporary monism is pure Spinozism.

Now, how do we conceive of this consciousness whose existence we are all so inclined to acknowledge? Impossible to define it, we are told, but we all have an immediate intuition of it: first of all, consciousness has consciousness of itself. Ask the first person you meet, man or woman, psychologist or layman, and he will answer you that he *feels himself* thinking, enjoying, suffering, desiring exactly as he feels himself breathing. He directly perceives his mental life as a sort of inner stream, active, light, fluid, delicate, diaphanous so to speak, and absolutely the opposite of anything material whatsoever. In short, the subjective life seems not merely to be a logically indispensable condition for the existence of an objective world which *appears;* it is also an element of the very experience which we sense directly, in the same way that we sense our own body.

Ideas and things, how can we fail to recognize their duality? Feelings and objects, how can we doubt their absolute heterogeneity?

The psychology that calls itself scientific acknowledges this heterogeneity just as the old spiritualist psychology acknowledged it. How can it not be acknowledged? Every science arbitrarily cuts out an area from the fabric of facts, an area to which it confines itself, and the content of which it describes and studies. Psychology takes for its domain precisely the area of facts of consciousness. It postulates them without criticizing them, it contrasts them with material facts; and without criticizing the notion of the latter, either, it connects them with consciousness through the mysterious link of *cognition* or *apperception,* which for psychology is a third sort of fundamental and ultimate fact. By following this path, contemporary psychology has celebrated great triumphs. It has been able to sketch the evolution of conscious life, conceiving the latter as adapting itself more and more completely to the physical milieu environing it. It has been able to establish a parallelism within the dualism, that of acts performed by the mind and events occurring in the brain. It has explained illusions, hallucinations, and, to a certain extent, mental illnesses. This is fine progress; but many more problems remain. General philosophy, above all, whose duty it is to scrutinize all postulates, finds paradoxes and obstacles in areas where science moves ahead without qualms; and it is only the fans of popular science who are never puzzled. The more deeply one goes into things, the more riddles are discovered; and I personally admit that, ever since I have been studying psychology seriously, that old duality of matter and thought, that heterogeneity of the two essences which is posited as being absolute, has always given me difficulties. It is of some of those difficulties that I would now like to speak to you.

First there is one which I am sure must have come to the

attention of all of you. Let us take perception of the outer world, the direct sensation we receive from the walls of this lecture hall, for example. Can we in this case say that the mental and the physical are absolutely heterogeneous? On the contrary, they are so far from being heterogeneous that if we take the common-sense viewpoint, if we disregard all explanatory inventions such as molecules and ether waves, which are basically metaphysical entities—if, in a word, we accept reality naïvely as it is given to us all at once, that able-to-be-sensed reality on which our vital interests depend and to which all our actions relate—well, that able-to-be-sensed reality and the sensation we have of it are, at the moment when the sensation is produced, absolutely identical to each other. Reality is apperception itself. The words "walls of this hall" merely signify this fresh, resonant whiteness surrounding us, interrupted by windows and bounded by these lines and angles. In this case the physical has no other content than the mental. Subject and object are merged.

Berkeley was the first to make this truth acclaimed. *Esse est percipi* [To be is to be perceived]. Our sensations are not small inner duplicates of things, they are the things themselves in so far as the things are present to us. And no matter what one may wish to think about the absent, hidden, and (so to speak) private life of things, and whatever one's hypothetical constructions of them may be, it remains true that the public life of things, that real presence with which they confront us, from which all our theoretical constructions are derived, and to which they must all return and reconnect themselves if they are not to float in the air and in irreality: that real presence, I say, is homogeneous, and not merely homogeneous, but also numerically one, with a certain part of our inner life.

So much for perception of the outer world. When we turn to imagination, memory, or the faculties of abstract representation, even though the facts here are much more complicated, I believe that the same essential homogeneity can be detected. To simplify the problem, let us first exclude

every type of reality that can be sensed. Let us consider
pure thought, as it takes place in dreams, daydreams, or
the memory of the past. Here, too, doesn't the stuff of experience do double duty? Don't the physical and the mental
merge? If I dream of a golden mountain, it no doubt does not
exist outside of my dream, but *in* my dream its nature or
essence is perfectly physical, it is *as* something physical
that it appears to me. If at this moment I allow myself to
recall my home in America and the details of my recent voyage to Italy, what is the pure phenomenon, the fact that is
produced? People say: it is my thought, with its content.
But, then, what is that content? It bears the form of a part
of the real world, a distant part, to be sure, involving six
thousand kilometers of space and six weeks of time, but still
a part of the world connected to this hall we are in by a
number of things, objects, and events which are homogeneous with the hall, on the one hand, and with the object of
my recollections, on the other.

This content does not present itself as being at first a
very small inner fact which I then project into the distance;
it presents itself at the very outset as the remote fact itself.
And what is the act of thinking this content? What is the
consciousness that I have of it? At bottom, are they anything other than retrospective ways of naming the content
itself, after separating it from all those physical intermediaries and connecting it to a new group of associates which
make it re-enter my mental life, for instance the emotions
it has aroused in me, the attention I am paying to it, my
ideas of a few moments ago which gave rise to it as a memory? It is only by becoming related to those last-named associates that the phenomenon can be classified as *thought;* all
the time that it relates only to the earlier ones, it remains
an *objective* phenomenon.

It is true that we usually contrast our inner images with
the objects, considering them as small copies, as weak trac-
ings or duplicates of the latter. This is because a present
object has a liveliness and clarity superior to those of the
image. Thus it contrasts with it; and, to use Taine's excel-

lent term, it serves as a "reductive" to it. When both are present together, the object occupies the foreground and the image "recedes," becomes an "absent" thing. But what is that present object in itself? Of what stuff is it made? Of the same stuff as the image. It is made of *sensations;* it is a thing perceived. Its *esse* is *percipi,* and it and the image are generically homogeneous.

If right now I think about my hat, which I left in the checkroom not long ago, where is the duality or the discontinuity between the thought-of hat and the real hat? My mind is occupied with a real *absent hat.* I take it into account in a practical manner, as I would a reality. If it were present on this table, the hat would determine a movement of my hand: I would take it away. Similarly, that conceptual hat, that hat in my thoughts, will before long determine the direction in which I walk. I will go and get it. The idea I have of it will continue until it leads to the able-to-be-sensed presence of the hat, and will merge with it harmoniously.

Therefore I conclude that—even though there is a practical duality, since images are distinguished from objects, take their place, and lead us to them—there is no reason to attribute to them an essential difference in nature. Thought and actuality are made of one and the same stuff, which is the stuff of experience in general.

The psychology of perception of the outer world leads us to the same conclusion. When I perceive the object in front of me as a table of a certain shape, at a certain distance, people explain to me that this fact is due to two factors: a matter that can be sensed which penetrates me by way of my eyes, supplying the element of real exteriority; and the ideas which are aroused, which confront that reality, classify it, and interpret it. But who, in the concretely apperceived table, can say what part is sensation and what part is idea? Outer and inner, extended and unextended, merge into an indissoluble combination. It reminds me of those circular panoramas in which such real objects as rocks, grass, broken wagons, etc., which occupy the foreground, are so ingeniously tied in with the painted canvas that constitutes the background, depicting a battle or a vast landscape, that we can no longer discern the solid objects from the painted ones. The seams and joinings are imperceptible.

Could that occur if object and idea were absolutely dissimilar in nature?

I am convinced that considerations such as those I have just expressed have already awakened in you, too, doubts concerning that alleged duality.

And other reasons for doubt come to mind. There is an entire sphere of adjectives and attributes which are neither objective nor subjective in an absolute way, but which we use now in one way, now in another, as if we enjoyed their ambiguity. I am speaking of the qualities that we *appreciate,* so to speak, in things, their æsthetic and moral side, their value for us. For example, wherein does beauty reside? Is it in the statue, in the sonata, or in our mind? My colleague at Harvard, George Santayana, has written a book on æsthetics[2] in which he calls beauty "pleasure objectified"; and, truly, it is surely in this case that we could speak of outward projection. We say without making discriminations "a pleasant warmth" or "a pleasant feeling of warmth." The rarity and preciousness of the diamond appear to us as essential qualities of it. We speak of a frightful storm, a hateful man, an ignoble action, and we think we are speaking objectively, even though those terms merely express relations to our own emotional sensitivity. We even say "a weary road," "a dismal sky," "a superb sunset." This whole animistic way of looking at things, which seems to have been mankind's primitive manner of thinking, can be explained very well (and Mr. Santayana, in another very recent book,[3] has well explained it in this way) by reference to our habit of attributing to the object *everything* that we feel in its presence. The distinction between subjective and objective is the result of

---

[2] *The Sense of Beauty,* pp. 44 ff.
[3] *The Life of Reason* [vol. I, "Reason in Common Sense," p. 142].

very advanced reflection, which we still like to postpone on
many occasions. When practical necessities do not draw us
out of it forcibly, we apparently enjoy indulging ourselves in
vagueness.

The secondary qualities themselves, heat, sound, light,
still have today only a vague attribution. For common
sense, for practical life, they are absolutely objective and
physical. For the physicist, they are subjective. For him,
only form, mass, and motion have an outer reality. For the
idealist philosopher, on the other hand, form and motion
are just as subjective as light and heat, and only the
unknown thing-in-itself, the "noumenon," enjoys complete
reality outside of the mind.

Our intimate sensations still retain some of that ambiguity. There are illusions of motion which prove that our earliest sensations of motion were generalized. The whole
world was moving with us. Now we distinguish our own
motion from that of the objects surrounding us, and among
the objects we single out some which remain at rest. But
there are conditions of lightheadedness in which even today
we relapse into that original failure to differentiate.

No doubt you are all familiar with the theory that tried to
make emotions summations of visceral and muscular sensations. It gave rise to many controversies, and no opinion
so far has been adhered to unanimously. You are also familiar with the controversies over the nature of mental activity. Some maintain that it is a purely spiritual force which
we are capable of apperceiving immediately as such. Others
claim that what we call mental activity (effort and attention, for example) is only the felt reflection of certain effects
seated in our organism, muscular tensions on the cranium
and throat, stoppage or free flow of respiration, rushes of
blood, etc.

In whatever manner these controversies will be resolved,
their existence proves one thing quite clearly: that it is very
difficult, or even absolutely impossible, to know by the mere
inner inspection of certain phenomena whether they are
physical in nature, possessing extension, etc., or whether

they are purely mental and inward in nature. We must always find reasons to support our opinion; we must look for the most likely classification of the phenomenon; and, in the end, we may very well find that all of our usual classifications had their motives in practical necessities rather than in some faculty we may possess of apperceiving two different ultimate essences which together might compose the complete fabric of things. The body of each one of us offers a practical contrast, which is almost violent, to all the rest of our ambient milieu. Everything that occurs inside that body is more intimate and important to us than what occurs elsewhere. It identifies itself with our ego, it classifies itself with it. Soul, life, breath—who can make a precise distinction between them? Even our images and our memories, which act on the physical world only by means of our body, seem to belong to it. We treat them as inner things, we classify them along with our affective feelings. To sum up, we are forced to admit that the question of the duality of thought and matter is far from being finally resolved.

And thereby ends the first part of my lecture. Ladies and gentlemen, I have attempted to instill in you my doubts and the reality, as well as the importance, of the problem.

As for me, after long years of hesitation, I have finally taken sides openly. I believe that consciousness, as we commonly conceive it, whether as an entity or as pure activity, but in both cases as being fluid, inextensive, diaphanous, and void of any content of its own, yet knowing itself directly—in a word, spiritual—I believe, I repeat, that this consciousness is a pure chimera, and that the sum of concrete realities which the word "consciousness" ought to encompass deserves a quite different description, a description, moreover, which a philosophy attentive to facts and capable of performing some analysis is by now able to supply or, rather, to begin to supply. And these words lead me to the second part of my lecture. It will be much shorter than the first part, because if I developed it on the same scale, it would be much too long. Therefore, I shall have to confine myself to the indispensable indications only.

*   *   *

Let us suppose that consciousness, *Bewusstheit,* conceived as an essence, entity, activity, or the irreducible half of every experience, is done away with, that the fundamental and, as it were, ontological dualism is eliminated, and that what we imagined as existent is merely what we have called up to now the content, the *Inhalt,* of the consciousness; how will philosophy cope with the sort of vague monism that will result? I shall try to afford you a few positive suggestions on that subject, even though I fear that, for want of the necessary development, my thoughts will not shed a very strong light. If only I can indicate the beginning of the path, that may be enough.

Basically, why do we cling so tenaciously to that notion of a consciousness which is superadded to the existence of the content of things? Why do we insist on it so forcefully that anyone who denies it seems more like a joker than a thinker to us? Is it not in order to safeguard that undeniable fact that the content of experience not only has an existence of its own, some immanent and intrinsic existence, but that each part of that content leaves its mark, so to speak, on its neighbors, giving an account of itself to others and, in some manner, going out of itself so it can be known; and that thus the whole field of experience is transparent from one end to another, or set up like a space filled with mirrors?

This biliterality of the parts of experience—that is, on the one hand, that they exist and have qualities of their own; on the other hand, that they stand in relation to other parts and are known—is recognized by prevailing opinion, which explains it by a fundamental duality of constitution belonging to every piece of experience in itself. In this sheet of paper, they say, there is not merely the content, whiteness, thinness, etc., but there is also the secondary fact of the consciousness of this whiteness and thinness. This function of being "related," of being a part of the entire fabric of a more comprehensive experience, is built up into an ontological fact, and they lodge this fact in the very interior of the paper, coupling it with its whiteness and thinness. It is not an extrinsic relation which is being postulated, it is a half of the phenomenon itself.

I believe that, in the final analysis, we conceive of reality as being constituted in the same way that the "paints" are made that we use in painting. First of all there are pigments, which correspond to the content, and then there is a solvent, oil or size, which keeps them in suspension and corresponds to the consciousness. This is a complete dualism in which, by using certain procedures, we can separate each element from the other by subtraction. It is thus that we are assured that, by making a great effort of introspective abstraction, we can put our finger directly on our consciousness, as on a pure spiritual activity, while disregarding more or less completely the matters which it illuminates at a given moment.

Now I ask you whether this way of seeing things cannot be absolutely reversed just as easily. Indeed, let us posit that the original reality is neutral in nature, and let us call it by some name that is still ambiguous, such as "phenomenon," "datum," or "*Vorfindung.*" As for me, I like to speak of it in the plural, and I give it the name of "pure experiences." This may be a type of monism, if you will, but a monism that is altogether rudimentary and in absolute contrast to that so-called bilateral monism of scientific or Spinozistic positivism.

These pure experiences exist and succeed one another; they enter into infinitely varied relations with one another, relations which are themselves essential parts of the fabric of experiences. There is "consciousness" of these relations just as there is "consciousness" of their terms. The result of this is that *groups* of experiences can be noticed and discerned, and that one and the same experience, given the great variety of its relations, can play a role in several groups at the same time. Thus it is that, in a certain context of neighbors, it may be classified as a physical phenomenon, while in different surroundings it may figure as a fact of consciousness, in approximately the same way that the same ink particle may belong simultaneously to two lines, one vertical and the other horizontal, as long as it is situated at their intersection.

To make our thoughts concrete, let us take the experience we have right now of the place we are in, of these walls, of this table, of these chairs, of this space. In this full, concrete, and undivided experience, such as it lies before us, as a given, the objective physical world and the personal inner world of each one of us meet and merge as lines merge at their intersection. As a physical thing this hall has relations to all the rest of the building, a building which *we* are not, and will not become, familiar with. The hall owes its existence to a long history of financiers, architects, workmen. It exerts weight on the ground; it will last for an indefinite time; if fire broke out in it, the chairs and table that it contains would quickly be reduced to ashes.

On the other hand, as a personal experience, as a thing that is "reported," known, and we are conscious of, this hall has quite other linkages. Its antecedents are not workmen, but our respective thoughts of a moment ago. Soon it will figure merely as a fleeting fact in our biographies, associated with pleasant memories. As a mental experience it has no weight, and its furnishings are not inflammable. The only physical force it exerts is on our brains, and many of us deny even that influence; whereas the physical hall has physically influenced relations with all the rest of the world.

And yet in both cases we are talking about absolutely the same hall. As long as we are not indulging in speculative physics but confining ourselves to common sense, it is the hall we see and feel that is certainly the physical hall. And so, what are we speaking about if not about *that,* that same part of material nature which all of our minds encompass at this same moment, which enters just as it stands into the actual, intimate experience of each one of us, and which our memory will always regard as an integral part of our history? It is absolutely one and the same stuff, which, depending on the context being considered, figures simultaneously as a material, physical fact or as a fact of inward consciousness.

Thus I believe that consciousness and matter cannot be handled as being of disparate essences. Neither one nor the other is obtained by subtraction, each time disregarding the other half of a doubly composed experience. On the contrary, experiences are originally of a rather noncomplex nature. They *become* part of our consciousness in their entirety, they *become* physical in their entirety; and this result is achieved *by addition*. To the extent that experiences are protracted in time and enter into physically influenced relations, breaking, heating, or illuminating one another, etc., we make a separate group out of them which we call the physical world. On the other hand, to the extent that they are transitory or physically inert, that their sequence does not follow a determined order but seems instead to obey emotional whims, we make another group out of them which we call the mental world. It is because at this moment it enters into a large number of these mental groups that this hall now becomes a thing we are conscious of, a reported, known thing. By becoming a part of our respective biographies from now on, it will not be followed by that silly and monotonous repetition of itself in time which characterizes its physical existence. On the contrary, it will be followed by other experiences which will be discontinuous with it, or which will have that very special sort of continuity we call "memory." Tomorrow it will have its place in the past of each one of us; but the various presents to which all those pasts will be linked tomorrow will be quite different from the present which this hall will enjoy tomorrow as a physical entity.

Both types of groups are formed of experiences, but the relations of the experiences among themselves differ from one group to the other. Thus it is by the addition of other phenomena that any given phenomenon enters our consciousness or becomes known; it is not by a self-division of an inner nature. The cognition of things comes to them from outside, it is not immanent in them. Neither a transcendental ego nor a *Bewusstheit* or act of consciousness would be able to animate each thing. *They know one another,* or, rather, some of them know the others; and the relation we call cognition is itself, in many cases, only a series of intermediate experiences perfectly susceptible of being described in concrete terms. In no way is it the transcendent mystery in which so many philosophers have delighted in believing.

But this would take us much too far. I cannot enter here into every detail of the theory of cognition, or of what you Italians call "gnosiology." I must be satisfied with these abridged remarks, or simple suggestions, which I fear are still quite obscure for want of the necessary developments.

Therefore, let me summarize—too briefly, and in a dogmatic way—with the following six propositions:

1. Consciousness, as it is commonly understood, does not exist, any more than does matter, to which Berkeley dealt the death blow.

2. What does exist, forming the portion of the truth encompassed by the word "consciousness," is the susceptibility possessed by the parts of experience of being reported or known.

3. This susceptibility can be explained by the fact that certain experiences can lead to others by way of clearly characterized intermediate experiences, so that some of them come to play the role of things known, and others that of knowers.

4. It is perfectly possible to define these two roles without departing from the fabric of experience itself and without invoking anything transcendental.

5. Therefore the attributions "subject" and "object," "represented" and "representing," "thing" and "thought," indicate a practical distinction which is of the utmost importance, but which is merely of a FUNCTIONAL order, in no way of an ontological order, as classical dualism conceives of it.

6. Lastly, things and thoughts are not fundamentally heterogeneous, but are made of the same stuff, a stuff which we cannot define as such but can merely sense, and which can be named, if we wish, the stuff of experience in general.

IX
Is Radical Empiricism Solipsistic?[1]

If all the criticisms which the humanistic *Weltanschauung* is receiving were as *sachgemäss* as Mr. Bode's,[2] the truth of the matter would more rapidly clear up. Not only is it excellently well written, but it brings its own point of view out clearly, and admits of a perfectly straight reply.

The argument (unless I fail to catch it) can be expressed as follows:

If a series of experiences be supposed, no one of which is endowed immediately with the self-transcendent function of reference to a reality beyond itself, no motive will occur within the series for supposing anything beyond it to exist. It will remain subjective, and contentedly subjective, both as a whole and in its several parts.

Radical empiricism, trying, as it does, to account for objective knowledge by means of such a series, egregiously fails. It can not explain how the notion of a physical order, as distinguished from a subjectively biographical order, of experiences, ever arose.

It pretends to explain the notion of a physical order, but does so by playing fast and loose with the concept of objective reference. On the one hand, it denies that such reference implies self-transcendency on the part of any one experience; on the other hand, it claims that experiences *point*. But, critically considered, there can be no pointing unless

---

[1] [Reprinted from *The Journal of Philosophy, Psychology and Scientific Methods,* vol. II, No. 9, April 27, 1905.]

[2] [B. H. Bode: "'Pure Experience' and the External World," *Journal of Philosophy, Psychology and Scientific Methods,* vol. II, 1905, p. 128.]

self-transcendency be also allowed. The conjunctive function of pointing, as I have assumed it, is, according to my
critic, vitiated by the fallacy of attaching a bilateral relation
to a term *a quo,* as if it could stick out substantively and
maintain itself in existence in advance of the term *ad quem*
which is equally required for it to be a concretely experienced fact. If the relation be made concrete, the term *ad
quem* is involved, which would mean (if I succeed in apprehending Mr. Bode rightly) that this latter term, although
not empirically there, is yet *noetically* there, in advance—in
other words it would mean that any experience that
"points" must already have transcended itself, in the ordinary "epistemological" sense of the word transcend.

Something like this, if I understand Mr. Bode's text, is
the upshot of his state of mind. It is a reasonable sounding
state of mind, but it is exactly the state of mind which radical empiricism, by its doctrine of the reality of conjunctive
relations, seeks to dispel. I very much fear—so difficult does
mutual understanding seem in these exalted regions—that
my able critic has failed to understand that doctrine as it is
meant to be understood. I suspect that he performs on all
these conjunctive relations (of which the aforesaid "pointing" is only one) the usual rationalistic act of substitution—
he takes them not as they are given in their first intention,
as parts constitutive of experience's living flow, but only as
they appear in retrospect, each fixed as a determinate
object of conception, static, therefore, and contained within
itself.

Against this rationalistic tendency to treat experience as
chopped up into discontinuous static objects, radical empiricism protests. It insists on taking conjunctions at their
"face-value," just as they come. Consider, for example, such
conjunctions as "and," "with," "near," *"plus,"* "towards."
While we live in such conjunctions our state is one of *transition* in the most literal sense. We are expectant of a "more"
to come, and before the more *has* come, the transition, nevertheless, is directed *towards* it. I fail otherwise to see how,
if one kind of more comes, there should be satisfaction and

feeling of fulfillment; but disappointment if the more comes in another shape. One more will continue, another more will arrest or deflect the direction, in which our experience is moving even now. We can not, it is true, *name* our different living "ands" or "withs" except by naming the different terms towards which they are moving us, but we *live* their specifications and differences before those terms explicitly arrive. Thus, though the various "ands" are all bilateral relations, each requiring a term *ad quem* to define it when viewed in retrospect and articulately conceived, yet in its living moment any one of them may be treated as if it "stuck out" from its term *a quo* and pointed in a special direction, much as a compass-needle (to use Mr. Bode's excellent simile) points at the pole, even though it stirs not from its box.

In Professor Höffding's massive little article in *The Journal of Philosophy, Psychology and Scientific Methods,*[3] he quotes a saying of Kierkegaard's to the effect that we live forwards, but we understand backwards. Understanding backwards is, it must be confessed, a very frequent weakness of philosophers, both of the rationalistic and of the ordinary empiricist type. Radical empiricism alone insists on understanding forwards also, and refuses to substitute static concepts of the understanding for transitions in our moving life. A logic similar to that which my critic seems to employ here should, it seems to me, forbid him to say that our present is, while present, directed towards our future, or that any physical movement can have direction until its goal is actually reached.

At this point does it not seem as if the quarrel about self-transcendency in knowledge might drop? Is it not a purely verbal dispute? Call it self-transcendency or call it pointing, whichever you like—it makes no difference so long as real transitions towards real goals are admitted as things given *in* experience, and among experience's most indefeasible parts. Radical empiricism, unable to close its eyes to the

---

[3] Vol. II, [1905], pp. 85–92.

transitions caught *in actu,* accounts for the self-transcendency or the pointing (whichever you may call it) as a process that occurs within experience, as an empirically mediated thing of which a perfectly definite description can be given. "Epistemology," on the other hand, denies this; and pretends that the self-transcendency is unmediated or, if mediated, then mediated in a super-empirical world. To justify this pretension, epistemology has first to transform all our conjunctions into static objects, and this, I submit, is an absolutely arbitrary act. But in spite of Mr. Bode's maltreatment of conjunctions, as I understand them—and as I understand him—I believe that at bottom we are fighting for nothing different, but are both defending the same continuities of experience in different forms of words.

There are other criticisms in the article in question, but, as this seems the most vital one, I will for the present, at any rate, leave them untouched.

X

MR. PITKIN'S REFUTATION OF "RADICAL EMPIRICISM"[1]

Although Mr. Pitkin does not name me in his acute article on radical empiricism,[2] [. . .] I fear that some readers, knowing me to have applied that name to my own doctrine, may possibly consider themselves to have been in at my death.

In point of fact my withers are entirely unwrung. I have, indeed, said[3] that "to be radical, an empiricism must not admit into its constructions any element that is not directly experienced." But in my own radical empiricism this is only a *methodological postulate,* not a conclusion supposed to flow from the intrinsic absurdity of transempirical objects. I have never felt the slightest respect for the idealistic arguments which Mr. Pitkin attacks and of which Ferrier made such striking use; and I am perfectly willing to admit any number of noumenal beings or events into philosophy if only their pragmatic value can be shown.

Radical empiricism and pragmatism have so many misunderstandings to suffer from, that it seems my duty not to let this one go any farther, uncorrected.

---

[1] [Reprinted from the *Journal of Philosophy, Psychology and Scientific Methods,* vol. III, No. 26, December 20, 1906; and *ibid.,* vol. IV, No. 4, February 14, 1907, where the original is entitled "A Reply to Mr. Pitkin." ED.]

[2] [W. B. Pitkin: "A Problem of Evidence in Radical Empiricism," *ibid.,* vol. III, No. 24, November 22, 1906. ED.]

[3] [In essay II above, "A World of Pure Experience," §I. ED.]

*   *   *

Mr. Pitkin's "reply" to me,[4] [. . .] perplexes me by the obscurity of style which I find in almost all our younger philosophers. He asks me, however, two direct questions which I understand, so I take the liberty of answering.

First he asks: Do not experience and science show "that countless things are[5] experienced *as* that which they are not or are only partially?" I reply: Yes, assuredly, as, for example, "things" distorted by refractive media, "molecules," or whatever else is taken to be more ultimately real than the immediate content of the perceptive moment.

Secondly: "If experience is self-supporting[6] (in *any* intelligible sense) does this fact preclude the possibility of (a) something not experienced and (b) action of experience upon a noumenon?"

My reply is: Assuredly not the possibility of either—how could it? Yet in my opinion we should be wise not to *consider* any thing or action of that nature, and to restrict our universe of philosophic discourse to what is experienced or, at least, experienceable.[7]

---

[4] ["In Reply to Professor James," *Journal of Philosophy, Psychology and Scientific Methods,* vol. IV, No. 2, January 17, 1907. Ed.]

[5] Mr. Pitkin inserts the clause: "by reason of the very nature of experience itself." Not understanding just what reason is meant, I do not include this clause in my answer.

[6] [See essay VII above, "The Essence of Humanism," §I. Ed.]

[7] [Elsewhere, in speaking of "reality" as "conceptual or perceptual experiences," the author says: "This is meant merely to exclude reality of an 'unknowable' sort, of which no account in either perceptual or conceptual terms can be given. It includes, of course, any amount of empirical reality independent of the knower." *Meaning of Truth,* p. 100, note. Ed.]

XI
Humanism and Truth Once More[1]

Mr. Joseph's criticism of my article "Humanism and Truth"[2] is a useful contribution to the general clearing up. He has seriously tried to comprehend what the pragmatic movement may intelligibly mean; and if he has failed, it is the fault neither of his patience nor of his sincerity, but rather of stubborn tricks of thought which he could not easily get rid of. Minute polemics, in which the parties try to rebut every detail of each of the other's charges, are a useful exercise only to the disputants. They can but breed confusion in a reader. I will therefore ignore as much as possible the text of both our articles (mine was inadequate enough) and treat once more the general objective situation.

As I apprehend the movement towards humanism, it is based on no particular discovery or principle that can be driven into one precise formula which thereupon can be impaled upon a logical skewer. It is much more like one of those secular changes that come upon public opinion overnight, as it were, borne upon tides "too full for sound or foam," that survive all the crudities and extravagances of their advocates, that you can pin to no one absolutely essential statement, nor kill by any one decisive stab.

---

[1] [Reprinted without change from *Mind,* N. S., vol. XIV, No. 54, April, 1905, pp. 190–198. Parts of this essay have also been reprinted in *The Meaning of Truth.* ED.]

[2] ["Humanism and Truth" first appeared in *Mind,* N. S., vol. XIII, No. 52, October, 1904. It is reprinted in *The Meaning of Truth,* pp. 51–101. Cf. this article *passim.* Mr. H. W. B. Joseph's criticism, entitled "Professor James on 'Humanism and Truth,'" appeared in *Mind,* N. S., vol. XIV, No. 53, January, 1905. ED.]

Such have been the changes from aristocracy to democracy, from classic to romantic taste, from theistic to pantheistic feeling, from static to evolutionary ways of understanding life—changes of which we all have been spectators. Scholasticism still opposes to such changes the method of confutation by single decisive reasons, showing that the new view involves self-contradiction, or traverses some fundamental principle. This is like stopping a river by planting a stick in the middle of its bed. Round your obstacle flows the water and "gets there all the same." In reading Mr. Joseph, I am not a little reminded of those Catholic writers who refute Darwinism by telling us that higher species can not come from lower because *minus nequit gignere plus,* or that the notion of transformation is absurd, for it implies that species tend to their own destruction, and that would violate the principle that every reality tends to persevere in its own shape. The point of view is too myopic, too tight and close to take in the inductive argument. You can not settle questions of fact by formal logic. I feel as if Mr. Joseph almost pounced on my words singly, without giving the sentences time to get out of my mouth.

The one condition of understanding humanism is to become inductive-minded oneself, to drop rigorous definitions, and follow lines of least resistance "on the whole." "In other words," Mr. Joseph may probably say, "resolve your intellect into a kind of slush." "Even so," I make reply,—"if you will consent to use no politer word." For humanism, conceiving the more "true" as the more "satisfactory" (Dewey's term) has to renounce sincerely rectilinear arguments and ancient ideals of rigor and finality. It is in just this temper of renunciation, so different from that of pyrrhonistic scepticism, that the spirit of humanism essentially consists. Satisfactoriness has to be measured by a multitude of standards, of which some, for aught we know, may fail in any given case; and what is "more" satisfactory than any alternative in sight, may to the end be a sum of *pluses* and *minuses,* concerning which we can only trust that by ulterior corrections and improvements a maximum of the one and a minimum of the other may some day be approached. It means a real change of heart, a break with absolutistic hopes, when one takes up this view of the conditions of belief.

That humanism's critics have never imagined this attitude inwardly, is shown by their invariable tactics. They do not get into it far enough to see objectively and from without what their own opposite notion of truth is. Mr. Joseph is possessed by some such notion; he thinks his readers to be full of it, he obeys it, works from it, but never even essays to tell us what it is. The nearest he comes to doing so is where[3] he says it is the way "we ought to think," whether we be psychologically compelled to or not.

Of course humanism agrees to this: it is only a manner of calling truth an ideal. But humanism explicates the summarizing word "ought" into a mass of pragmatic motives from the midst of which our critics think that truth itself takes flight. Truth is a name of double meaning. It stands now for an abstract something defined only as that to which our thought ought to conform; and again it stands for the concrete propositions within which we believe that conformity already reigns—they being so many "truths." Humanism sees that the only conformity we ever have to deal with concretely is that between our subjects and our predicates, using these words in a very broad sense. It sees moreover that this conformity is "validated" (to use Mr. Schiller's term) by an indefinite number of pragmatic tests that vary as the predicates and subjects vary. If an S gets superseded by an SP that gives our mind a completer sum of satisfactions, we always say, humanism points out, that we have advanced to a better position in regard to truth.

Now many of our judgments thus attained are retrospective. The S'es, so the judgment runs, were SP's already ere the fact was humanly recorded. Common sense, struck by this state of things, now rearranges the whole field; and traditional philosophy follows her example. The general

---

[3] *Op. cit.,* p. 37.

requirement that predicates must conform to their subject, they translate into an ontological theory. A most previous Subject of all is substituted for the lesser subjects and conceived of as an archetypal Reality; and the conformity required of predicates in detail is reinterpreted as a relation which our whole mind, with all its subjects and predicates together, must get into with respect to this Reality. It, meanwhile, is conceived as eternal, static, and unaffected by our thinking. Conformity to a non-human Archetype like this is probably the notion of truth which my opponent shares with common sense and philosophic rationalism.

When now Humanism, fully admitting both the naturalness and the grandeur of this hypothesis, nevertheless points to its sterility, and declines to chime in with the substitution, keeping to the concrete and still lodging truth between the subjects and the predicates in detail, it provokes the outcry which we hear and which my critic echoes.

One of the commonest parts of the outcry is that humanism is subjectivistic altogether—it is supposed to labor under a necessity of "denying trans-perceptual reality."[4] It is not hard to see how this misconception of humanism may have arisen; and humanistic writers, partly from not having sufficiently guarded their expressions, and partly from not having yet "got round" (in the poverty of their literature) to a full discussion of the subject, are doubtless in some degree to blame. But I fail to understand how any one with a working grasp of their principles can charge them wholesale with subjectivism. I myself have never thought of humanism as being subjectivistic farther than to this extent, that, inasmuch as it treats the thinker as being himself one portion of reality, it must also allow that *some* of the realities that he declares for true are created by his being there. Such realities of course are either acts of his, or relations between other things and him, or relations between things, which, but for him, would never have been traced.

---

[4] [Cf. essay X above, "Mr. Pitkin's Refutation. . . ."]

Humanists are subjectivistic, also in this, that, unlike rationalists (who think they carry a warrant for the absolute truth of what they now believe in in their present pocket), they hold all present beliefs as subject to revision in the light of future experience. The future experience, however, may be of things outside the thinker; and that this is so the humanist may believe as freely as any other kind of empiricist philosopher.

The critics of humanism (though here I follow them but darkly) appear to object to any infusion whatever of subjectivism into truth. All must be archetypal; every truth must pre-exist to its perception. Humanism sees that an enormous quantity of truth must be written down as having pre-existed to its perception of us humans. In countless instances we find it most satisfactory to believe that, though we were always ignorant of the fact, it always *was* a fact that S was SP. But humanism separates this class of cases from those in which it is more satisfactory to believe the opposite, e.g., that S is ephemeral, or P a passing event, or SP created by the perceiving act. Our critics seem on the other hand, to wish to universalize the retrospective type of instance. Reality must pre-exist to every assertion for which truth is claimed. And, not content with this overuse of one particular type of judgment, our critics claim its monopoly. They appear to wish to cut off Humanism from its rights to any retrospection at all.

Humanism says that satisfactoriness is what distinguishes the true from the false. But satisfactoriness is both a subjective quality, and a present one. *Ergo* (the critics appear to reason) an object, *quâ* true, must always for humanism be both present and subjective, and a humanist's belief can never be in anything that lives outside of the belief itself or antedates it. Why so preposterous a charge should be so current, I find it hard to say. Nothing is more obvious than the fact that both the objective and the past existence of the object may be the very things about it that most seem satisfactory, and that most invite us to believe them. The past tense can figure in the humanist's world, as well of belief as of representation, quite as harmoniously as in the world of any one else.

Mr. Joseph gives a special turn to this accusation. He charges me[5] with being self-contradictory when I say that the main categories of thought were evolved in the course of experience itself. For I use these very categories to define the course of experience by. Experience, as I talk about it, is a product of their use; and yet I take it as true anteriorly to them. This seems to Mr. Joseph to be an absurdity. I hope it does not seem such to his readers; for if experiences can suggest hypotheses at all (and they notoriously do so) I can see no absurdity whatever in the notion of a retrospective hypothesis having for its object the very train of experiences by which its own being, along with that of other things, has been brought about. If the hypothesis is "satisfactory" we must, of course, believe it to have been true anteriorly to its formulation by ourselves. Every explanation of a present by a past seems to involve this kind of circle, which is not a vicious circle. The past is *causa existendi* of the present, which in turn is *causa cognoscendi* of the past. If the present were treated as *causa existendi* of the past, the circle might indeed be vicious.

Closely connected with this pseudo-difficulty is another one of wider scope and greater complication—more excusable therefore.[6] Humanism, namely, asking how truth in point of fact is reached, and seeing that it is by ever substituting more satisfactory for less satisfactory opinions, is thereby led into a vague historic sketch of truth's development. The earliest "opinions," it thinks, must have been dim, unconnected "feelings," and only little by little did more and more orderly views of things replace them. Our own retrospective view of this whole evolution is now, let us say, the latest candidate for "truth" as yet reached in the process. To be a satisfactory candidate, it must give some definite sort of a picture of what forces keep the process

---

[5] *Op. cit.*, p. 32.

[6] [This] Mr. Joseph deals with (though in much too pettifogging and logic-chopping a way) on pp. 33–34 of his article.

going. On the subjective side we have a fairly definite picture—sensation, association, interest, hypothesis, these account in a general way for the growth into a cosmos of the relative chaos with which the mind began.

But on the side of the object, so to call it roughly, our view is much less satisfactory. Of which of our many objects are we to believe that it truly *was* there and at work before the human mind began? Time, space, kind, number, serial order, cause, consciousness, are hard things not to objectify—even transcendental idealism leaves them standing as "empirically real." Substance, matter, force, fall down more easily before criticism, and secondary qualities make almost no resistance at all. Nevertheless, when we survey the field of speculation, from Scholasticism through Kantism to Spencerism, we find an ever-recurring tendency to convert the pre-human into a merely logical object, an unknowable *ding-an-sich,* that but starts the process, or a vague *materia prima* that but receives our forms.[7]

The reasons for this are not so much logical as they are material. We can postulate an extra-mental *that* freely enough (though some idealists have denied us the privilege), but when we have done so, the *what* of it is hard to determine satisfactorily, because of the oppositions and entanglements of the variously proposed *whats* with one another and with the history of the human mind. The literature of speculative cosmology bears witness to this difficulty. Humanism suffers from it no more than any other philosophy suffers, but it makes all our cosmogonic theories so unsatisfactory that some thinkers seek relief in the denial of any primal dualism. Absolute Thought or "pure experience" is postulated, and endowed with attributes calculated to justify the belief that it may "run itself." Both these truth-claiming hypotheses are non-dualistic in the old mind-and-matter sense; but the one is monistic and the other pluralistic as to the world process itself. Some humanists are non-

---

[7] Compare some elaborate articles by M. Le Roy and M. Wilbois in the *Revue de Métaphysique et de Morale,* vols. VIII, IX, and X, [1900, 1901, and 1902.]

dualists of this sort—I myself am one *und zwar* of the pluralistic brand. But doubtless dualistic humanists also exist,
as well as non-dualistic ones of the monistic wing.

Mr. Joseph pins these general philosophic difficulties on
humanism alone, or possibly on me alone. My article spoke
vaguely of a "most chaotic pure experience" coming first,
and building up the mind.[8] But how can two structureless
things interact so as to produce a structure? my critic tri-
umphantly asks. Of course they can't, as purely so-named
entities. We must make additional hypotheses. We must
beg a minimum of structure for them. The *kind* of minimum
that *might* have tended to increase towards what we now
find actually developed is the philosophical desideratum
here. The question is that of the most materially satisfactory hypothesis. Mr. Joseph handles it by formal logic
purely, as if he had no acquaintance with the logic of
hypothesis at all.

Mr. Joseph again is much bewildered as to what a
humanist can mean when he uses the word knowledge. He
tries to convict me of vaguely identifying it with any kind of
good. Knowledge is a difficult thing to define briefly, and
Mr. Joseph shows his own constructive hand here even less
than in the rest of his article. I have myself put forth on several occasions a radically pragmatist account of knowledge,[9] the existence of which account my critic probably
does not know of—so perhaps I had better not say anything
about knowledge until he reads and attacks that. I will say,
however, that whatever the relation called knowing may
itself prove to consist in, I can think of no conceivable kind
of *object* which may not become an object of knowledge on
humanistic principles as well as on the principles of any
other philosophy.[10]

---

[8] [Cf. *The Meaning of Truth,* p. 64.]

[9] Most recently in two articles, "Does 'Consciousness' Exist?" and "A
World of Pure Experience." [See essays I and II above.]

[10] For a recent attempt, effective on the whole, at squaring humanism
with knowing, I may refer to Prof. Woodbridge's very able address at
the Saint Louis Congress, "The Field of Logic," printed in *Science,* N. Y.,
November 4, 1904.

I confess that I am pretty steadily hampered by the habit, on the part of humanism's critics, of assuming that they have truer ideas than mine of truth and knowledge, the nature of which I must know of and can not need to have re-defined. I have consequently to reconstruct these ideas in order to carry on the discussion (I have e.g. had to do so in some parts of this article) and I thereby expose myself to charges of caricature. In one part of Mr. Joseph's attack, however, I rejoice that we are free from this embarrass-ment. It is an important point and covers probably a gen-uine difficulty, so I take it up last.

When, following Schiller and Dewey, I define the true as that which gives the maximal combination of satisfactions, and say that satisfaction is a many-dimensional term that can be realized in various ways, Mr. Joseph replies, rightly enough, that the chief satisfaction of a rational creature must always be his thought that what he believes is *true,* whether the truth brings him the satisfaction of collateral profits or not. This would seem, however, to make of truth the prior concept, and to relegate satisfaction to a secondary place.

Again, if to be satisfactory is what is meant by being true, *whose* satisfactions, and *which* of his satisfactions, are to count? Discriminations notoriously have to be made; and the upshot is that only rational candidates and intellectual sat-isfactions stand the test. We are then driven to a purely the-oretic notion of truth, and get out of the pragmatic atmos-phere altogether. And with this Mr. Joseph leaves us—truth is truth, and there is an end of the matter. But he makes a very pretty show of convicting me of self-stultification in according to our purely theoretic satisfactions any place in the humanistic scheme. They crowd the collateral satisfac-tions out of house and home, he thinks, and pragmatism has to go into bankruptcy if she recognizes them at all.

There is no room for disagreement about the facts here; but the destructive force of the reasoning disappears as soon as we talk concretely instead of abstractly, and ask, in our quality of good pragmatists, just what the famous theo-retic needs are known as and in what the intellectual satisfactions consist. Mr. Joseph, faithful to the habits of his party, makes no attempt at characterizing them, but assumes that their nature is self-evident to all.

Are they not all mere matters of *consistency*—and emphatically *not* of consistency between an Absolute Reality and the mind's copies of it, but of actually felt consistency among judgments, objects, and manners of reacting, in the mind? And are not both our need of such consistency and our pleasure in it conceivable as outcomes of the natural fact that we are beings that develop mental *habits*—habit itself proving adaptively beneficial in an environment where the same objects, or the same kinds of objects, recur and follow "law"? If this were so, what would have come first would have been the collateral profits of habit, and the theoretic life would have grown up in aid of these. In point of fact this seems to have been the probable case. At life's origin, any present perception may have been "true"—if such a word could then be applicable. Later, when reactions became organized, the reactions became "true" whenever expectation was fulfilled by them. Otherwise they were "false" or "mistaken" reactions. But the same class of objects needs the same kind of reaction, so the impulse to react consistently must gradually have been established, with a disappointment felt whenever the results frustrated expectation. Here is a perfectly plausible germ for all our higher consistencies. Nowadays, if an object claims from us a reaction of the kind habitually accorded only to the opposite class of objects, our mental machinery refuses to run smoothly. The situation is intellectually unsatisfactory. To gain relief we seek either to preserve the reaction by re-interpreting the object, or, leaving the object as it is, we react in a way contrary to the way claimed of us. Neither solution is easy. Such a situation might be that of Mr. Joseph, with me claiming assent to humanism from him. He can not apperceive it so as to permit him to gratify my claim; but there is enough appeal in the claim to induce him to write a whole article in justification of his refusal. If he should assent to humanism, on the other hand, that would drag after it an unwelcome, yea incredible, alteration of his previous mental beliefs. Whichever alternative he might adopt, however, a new equilibrium of intellectual consistency would in the end be reached. He would feel, whichever way he decided, that he was now thinking truly. But if, with his old habits unaltered, he should simply add to them the new one of advocating humanism quietly or noisily, his mind would be rent into two systems, each of which would accuse the other of falsehood. The resultant situation, being profoundly unsatisfactory, would also be instable.

Theoretic truth is thus no relation between our mind and archetypal reality. It falls *within* the mind, being the accord of some of its processes and objects with other processes and objects—"accord" consisting here in well-definable relations. So long as the satisfaction of feeling such an accord is denied us, whatever collateral profits may seem to inure from what we believe in are but as dust in the balance—provided always that we are highly organized intellectually, which the majority of us are not. The amount of accord which satisfies most men and women is merely the absence of violent clash between their usual thoughts and statements and the limited sphere of sense-perceptions in which their lives are cast. The theoretic truth that most of us think we "ought" to attain to is thus the possession of a set of predicates that do not contradict their subjects. We preserve it as often as not by leaving other predicates and subjects out.

In some men theory is a passion, just as music is in others. The form of inner consistency is pursued far beyond the line at which collateral profits stop. Such men systematize and classify and schematize and make synoptical tables and invent ideal objects for the pure love of unifying. Too often the results, glowing with "truth" for the inventors, seem pathetically personal and artificial to bystanders. Which is as much as to say that the purely theoretic criterion of truth can leave us in the lurch as easily as any other criterion.

I think that if Mr. Joseph will but consider all these things a little more concretely, he may find that the humanistic scheme and the notion of theoretic truth fall into line consistently enough to yield him also intellectual satisfaction.

XII
ABSOLUTISM AND EMPIRICISM[1]

No seeker of truth can fail to rejoice at the terre-à-terre sort of discussion of the issues between Empiricism and Transcendentalism (or, as the champions of the latter would probably prefer to say, between Irrationalism and Rationalism) that seems to have begun in *Mind.*[2] It would seem as if, over concrete examples like Mr. J. S. Haldane's, both parties ought inevitably to come to a better understanding. As a reader with a strong bias towards Irrationalism, I have studied his article[3] with the liveliest admiration of its temper and its painstaking effort to be clear. But the cases discussed failed to satisfy me, and I was at first tempted to write a Note animadverting upon them in detail. The growth of the limb, the sea's contour, the vicarious functioning of the nerve-centre, the digitalis curing the heart, are unfortunately *not* cases where we can *see* any *through-and-through* conditioning of the parts by the whole. They are all cases of reciprocity where subjects, supposed independently to exist, acquire certain attributes through their relations to other subjects. That they also *exist* through similar relations is only an ideal supposition, not verified to our understanding in these or any other concrete cases whatsoever.

If, however, one were to urge this solemnly, Mr. Haldane's friends could easily reply that he only gave us such examples on account of the hardness of our hearts. He knew full

---

[1] [Reprinted from *Mind,* vol. IX, No. 34, April, 1884.]
[2] [In 1884.]
[3] ["Life and Mechanism," *Mind,* vol. IX, 1884.]

well their imperfection, but he hoped that to those who would not spontaneously ascend to the Notion of the Totality, these cases might prove a spur and suggest and symbolize something better than themselves. No particular case that can be brought forward is a real concrete. They are all abstractions from the Whole, and of course the "through-and-through" character can not be found in them. Each of them still contains among its elements what we call *things,* grammatical subjects, forming a sort of residual *caput mortuum* of Existence after all the relations that figure in the examples have been told off. On this "existence," thinks popular philosophy, things may live on, like the winter bears on their own fat, never entering relations at all, or, if entering them, entering an entirely different set of them from those treated of in Mr. Haldane's examples. Thus *if* the digitalis were to weaken instead of strengthening the heart, and to produce death (as sometimes happens), it would determine itself, through determining the organism, to the function of "kill" instead of that of "cure." The function and relation seem adventitious, depending on what kind of a heart the digitalis gets hold of, the digitalis and the heart being facts external and, so to speak, accidental to each other. But this popular view, Mr. Haldane's friends will continue, is an illusion. What seems to us the "existence" of digitalis and heart outside of the relations of killing or curing, is but a function in a wider system of relations, of which, *pro hac vice,* we take no account. The larger system determines the *existence* just as absolutely as the system "kill," or the system "cure," determined the *function* of the digitalis. Ascend to the absolute system, instead of biding with these relative and partial ones, and you shall see that the law of through-and-throughness must and does obtain.

Of course, this argument is entirely reasonable, and debars us completely from chopping logic about the concrete examples Mr. Haldane has chosen. It is not his fault if his categories are so fine an instrument that nothing but the sum total of things can be taken to show us the manner of their use. It is simply our misfortune that he has not the sum total of things to show it by. Let us fall back from all concrete attempts and see what we can do with his notion of through-and-throughness, avowedly taken *in abstracto*. In abstract systems the "through-and-through" Ideal is realized on every hand. In any system, as such, the members are only *members* in the system. Abolish the system and you abolish its members, for you have conceived them through no other property than the abstract one of membership. Neither rightness nor leftness, except through bilaterality. Neither mortgager nor mortgagee, except through mortgage. The logic of these cases is this:—*If* A, then B; but *if* B, then A: wherefore *if* either, Both; and if not Both, Nothing.

It costs nothing, not even a mental effort, to admit that the absolute totality of things *may* be organized exactly after the pattern of one of these "through-and-through" abstractions. In fact, it is the pleasantest and freest of mental movements. Husband makes, and is made by, wife, through marriage; one makes other, by being itself other; everything self-created through its opposite—you go round like a squirrel in a cage. But if you stop and reflect upon what you are about, you lay bare the exact point at issue between common sense and the "through-and-through" school.

What, in fact, is the logic of these abstract systems? It is, as we said above: If any Member, then the Whole System; if not the Whole System, then Nothing. But how can Logic possibly do anything more with these two hypotheses than combine them into the single disjunctive proposition— "Either this Whole System, just as it stands, or Nothing at all." Is not that disjunction the ultimate word of Logic in the matter, and can any disjunction, as such, resolve *itself*? It may be that Mr. Haldane sees how one horn, the concept of the Whole System, carries real existence with it. But if he has been as unsuccessful as I in assimilating the Hegelian re-editings of the Anselmian proof, he will have to say that though Logic may determine *what* the system must be, *if* it is, something else than Logic must tell us *that* it is. Mr.

Haldane in this case would probably consciously, or unconsciously, make an appeal to Fact: the disjunction *is* decided, since nobody can dispute that now, as a matter of fact, *something,* and not nothing, *is.* We must *therefore,* he would probably say, go on to admit the Whole System in the desiderated sense. Is not then the validity of the Anselmian proof the nucleus of the whole question between Logic and Fact? Ought not the efforts of Mr. Haldane and his friends to be principally devoted to its elucidation? Is it not the real door of separation between Empiricism and Rationalism? And if the Rationalists leave that door for a moment off its hinges, can any power keep that abstract, opaque, unmediated, external, irrational, and irresponsible monster, known to the vulgar as bare Fact, from getting in and contaminating the whole sanctuary with his presence? Can anything prevent Faust from changing "Am Anfang war das Wort" into "Am Anfang war die That"?

Nothing in earth or heaven. Only the Anselmian proof can keep Fact out of philosophy. The question, "Shall Fact be recognized as an ultimate principle?" is the whole issue between the Rationalists and the Empiricism of vulgar thought.

Of course, if so recognized, Fact sets a limit to the "through-and-through" character of the world's rationality. That rationality might then mediate between all the members of our conception of the world, but not between the conception itself and reality. Reality would have to be given, not by Reason, but by Fact. Fact holds out blankly, brutally and blindly, against that universal deliquescence of everything into logical relations which the Absolutist Logic demands, and it is the only thing that does hold out. Hence the ire of the Absolutist Logic—hence its non-recognition, its "cutting" of Fact.

The reasons it gives for the "cutting" are that Fact is speechless, a mere word for the negation of thought, a vacuous unknowability, a dog-in-the-manger, in truth, which having no rights of its own, can find nothing else to do than to keep its betters out of theirs.

There are two points involved here: first the claim that certain things have rights that are absolute, ubiquitous and all pervasive, and in regard to which nothing else can possibly exist in its *own* right; and second that anything that denies *this* assertion is *pure* negativity with no positive context whatsoever.

Take the latter point first. Is it true that what is negative in one way is thereby convicted of incapacity to be positive in any other way? The word "Fact" is like the word "Accident," like the word "Absolute" itself. They all have their negative connotation. In truth, their whole connotation is negative and relative. All it says is that, whatever the thing may be that is denoted by the words, *other* things do not control it. Where fact, where accident is, they must be silent, it alone can speak. But that does not prevent its speaking as loudly as you please, in its own tongue. It may have an inward life, self-transparent and active in the maximum degree. An indeterminate future volition on my part, for example, would be a strict accident as far as my present self is concerned. But that could not prevent it, *in the moment in which it occurred,* from being possibly the most intensely living and luminous experience I ever had. Its quality of being a brute fact *ab extra* says nothing whatever as to its inwardness. It simply says to *outsiders:* "Hands off!"

And this brings us back to the first point of the Absolutist indictment of Fact. Is that point really anything more than a fantastic dislike to letting *anything* say "Hands off"? What else explains the contempt the Absolutist authors exhibit for a freedom defined simply on its "negative" side, as freedom "from," etc.? What else prompts them to deride such freedom? But, dislike for dislike, who shall decide? Why is not their dislike at having me "from" them, entirely on a par with mine at having them "through" me?

I know very well that in talking of dislikes to those who never mention them, I am doing a very coarse thing, and making a sort of intellectual Orson of myself. But, for the life of me, I can not help it, because I feel sure that likes and dislikes *must* be among the ultimate factors of their philosophy as well as of mine. Would they but admit it! How sweetly we then could hold converse together! There is something finite about us both, as we now stand. We do not know the Absolute Whole *yet*. *Part* of it is still negative to us. Among the *whats* of it still stalks a mob of opaque *thats*, without which we cannot think. But just as I admit that this is all possibly provisional, that even the Anselmian proof may come out all right, and creation *may* be a rational system through-and-through, why might they not also admit that it may all be otherwise, and that the shadow, the opacity, the negativity, the "from"-ness, the plurality that is ultimate, *may* never be wholly driven from the scene. We should both then be avowedly making hypotheses, playing with Ideals. Ah! Why is the notion of hypothesis so abhorrent to the Hegelian mind?

And once down on our common level of hypothesis, we might then admit scepticism, since the Whole is not yet revealed, to be the soundest *logical* position. But since we are in the main not sceptics, we might go on and frankly confess to each other the motives for our several faiths. I frankly confess mine—I can not but think that at bottom they are of an æsthetic and not of a logical sort. The "through-and-through" universe seems to suffocate me with its infallible impeccable all-pervasiveness. Its necessity, with no possibilities; its relations, with no subjects, make me feel as if I had entered into a contrast with no reserved rights, or rather as if I had to live in a large seaside boarding-house with no private bed-room in which I might take refuge from the society of the place. I am distinctly aware, moreover, that the old quarrel of sinner and pharisee has something to do with the matter. Certainly, to my personal knowledge, all Hegelians are not prigs, but I somehow feel as if all prigs ought to end, if developed, by becoming Hegelians. There is a story of two clergymen asked by mistake to conduct the same funeral. One came first and had got no farther than "I am the Resurrection and the Life," when the other entered. "*I* am the Resurrection and the

Life," cried the latter. The "through-and-through" philosophy, as it actually exists, reminds many of us of that cler-
gyman. It seems too buttoned-up and white-chokered and
clean-shaven a thing to speak for the vast slow-breathing
unconscious Kosmos with its dread abysses and its
unknown tides. The "freedom" *we* want to see there is not
the freedom, with a string tied to its leg and warranted not
to fly away, of that philosophy. "Let it fly away," we say,
"from *us!* What then?"

Again, I know I am exhibiting my mental grossness. But
again, *Ich kann nicht anders.* I show my feelings; why *will*
they not show theirs? I know they *have* a personal feeling
about the through-and-through universe, which is entirely
different from mine, and which I should very likely be much
the better for gaining if they would only show me how. Their
persistence in telling me that feeling has nothing to do with
the question, that it is a pure matter of absolute reason,
keeps me for ever out of the pale. Still seeing a *that* in
things which Logic does not expel, the most I can do is to
aspire to the expulsion. At present I do not even aspire.
Aspiration is a feeling. What can kindle feeling but the
example of feeling? And if the Hegelians *will* refuse to set
an example, what can they expect the rest of us to do? To
speak more seriously, the one *fundamental* quarrel
Empiricism has with Absolutism is over this repudiation by
Absolutism of the personal and æsthetic factor in the construction of philosophy. That we all of us have feelings,
Empiricism feels quite sure. That they may be as prophetic
and anticipatory of truth as anything else we have, and
some of them more so than others, can not possibly be
denied. But what hope is there of squaring and settling
opinions unless Absolutism will hold parley on this common
ground; and will admit that all philosophies are hypotheses, to which all our faculties, emotional as well as logical,
help us, and the truest of which will at the final integration
of things be found in possession of the men whose faculties
on the whole had the best divining power?

INDEX

Absolute Idealism: 25, 31, 52, 53, 70, 103, 135ff, Essay XII.
Activity: vii, Essay VI.
Affectional Facts: 18ff, Essay V, 115ff.
Agnosticism: 102.
Appreciations. *See* Affectional Facts.

Bergson, H.: 81, 99.
Berkeley: 6, 23, 40, 112, 122.
Bode, B. H.: 123ff.
Body: 41, 44ff, 80, 117.
Bradley, F. H.: 32, 51, 52, 55ff, 82, 84.

Cause: 85, 91, 95ff.
Change: 84.
Cognitive Relation: 27ff. *See also* Knowledge.
Concepts: 8ff, 11, 18, 29ff, 34ff.
Conjunctive Relations: vi, 24ff, 31, 37, 49, 54, 56ff, 61ff, 85, 126.
Consciousness: vii, Essay I, 39, 42, 67ff, 73ff, 80, 96, Essay VIII.
Continuity: 25ff, 31, 37, 49.

Democritus: 6.
Descartes: 16.
Dewey, J.: 28, 81, 101, 108, 130, 137.
Disjunctive Relations: vi, 23ff, 54, 56ff.
Dualism: 5, 110ff, 119, 135.

Empiricism: iii–viii, 22, 25, Essay XII. *See also* Radical Empiricism.
Epistemology: 126. *See also* Knowledge.
Ethics: 102.
Experience: v, vii, 4ff, 28, 33ff, 37, 42, 45, 48, 114, 118, 122, 128. *See also* Pure Experience.
External Relations: 57ff. *See also* Relations, and Disjunctive.

Feeling. *See* Affectional Facts.
Free Will: 97.

Haldane, J. S.: 140ff.
Hegel: 55, 145.
Herbart: 55.
Hobhouse, L. T.: 57.
Hodder, A. L.: 11, 57.
Hodgson, S.: vi, 25.
Höffding, H.: 125.
Humanism: 47, 81, Essay VII, Essay XI.
Hume: vii, 22, 23, 54, 91.

Idealism: 21, 71, 116, 127, 135.
Ideas: 29ff, 38, 93, 11.
Identity, Philosophy of: 71, 104, 106.
Indeterminism: 47, 144.
Intellect: 50ff.

Joseph, H. W. B.: 107, 129ff.

147

A CATALOG OF SELECTED
DOVER BOOKS
IN ALL FIELDS OF INTEREST

A CATALOG OF SELECTED DOVER
BOOKS IN ALL FIELDS OF INTEREST

CONCERNING THE SPIRITUAL IN ART, Wassily Kandinsky. Pioneering work by father of abstract art. Thoughts on color theory, nature of art. Analysis of earlier masters. 12 illustrations. 80pp. of text. 5⅜ x 8½.   23411-8

ANIMALS: 1,419 Copyright-Free Illustrations of Mammals, Birds, Fish, Insects, etc., Jim Harter (ed.). Clear wood engravings present, in extremely lifelike poses, over 1,000 species of animals. One of the most extensive pictorial sourcebooks of its kind. Captions. Index. 284pp. 9 x 12.   23766-4

CELTIC ART: The Methods of Construction, George Bain. Simple geometric techniques for making Celtic interlacements, spirals, Kells-type initials, animals, humans, etc. Over 500 illustrations. 160pp. 9 x 12. (Available in U.S. only.)   22923-8

AN ATLAS OF ANATOMY FOR ARTISTS, Fritz Schider. Most thorough reference work on art anatomy in the world. Hundreds of illustrations, including selections from works by Vesalius, Leonardo, Goya, Ingres, Michelangelo, others. 593 illustrations. 192pp. 7⅛ x 10¼.   20241-0

CELTIC HAND STROKE-BY-STROKE (Irish Half-Uncial from "The Book of Kells"): An Arthur Baker Calligraphy Manual, Arthur Baker. Complete guide to creating each letter of the alphabet in distinctive Celtic manner. Covers hand position, strokes, pens, inks, paper, more. Illustrated. 48pp. 8¼ x 11.   24336-2

EASY ORIGAMI, John Montroll. Charming collection of 32 projects (hat, cup, pelican, piano, swan, many more) specially designed for the novice origami hobbyist. Clearly illustrated easy-to-follow instructions insure that even beginning papercrafters will achieve successful results. 48pp. 8¼ x 11.   27298-2

THE COMPLETE BOOK OF BIRDHOUSE CONSTRUCTION FOR WOODWORKERS, Scott D. Campbell. Detailed instructions, illustrations, tables. Also data on bird habitat and instinct patterns. Bibliography. 3 tables. 63 illustrations in 15 figures. 48pp. 5¼ x 8½.   24407-5

BLOOMINGDALE'S ILLUSTRATED 1886 CATALOG: Fashions, Dry Goods and Housewares, Bloomingdale Brothers. Famed merchants' extremely rare catalog depicting about 1,700 products: clothing, housewares, firearms, dry goods, jewelry, more. Invaluable for dating, identifying vintage items. Also, copyright-free graphics for artists, designers. Co-published with Henry Ford Museum & Greenfield Village. 160pp. 8¼ x 11.   25780-0

HISTORIC COSTUME IN PICTURES, Braun & Schneider. Over 1,450 costumed figures in clearly detailed engravings—from dawn of civilization to end of 19th century. Captions. Many folk costumes. 256pp. 8⅜ x 11¾.   23150-X

STICKLEY CRAFTSMAN FURNITURE CATALOGS, Gustav Stickley and L. & J. G. Stickley. Beautiful, functional furniture in two authentic catalogs from 1910. 594 illustrations, including 277 photos, show settles, rockers, armchairs, reclining chairs, bookcases, desks, tables. 183pp. 6½ x 9¼.   23838-5

AMERICAN LOCOMOTIVES IN HISTORIC PHOTOGRAPHS: 1858 to 1949, Ron Ziel (ed.). A rare collection of 126 meticulously detailed official photographs, called "builder portraits," of American locomotives that majestically chronicle the rise of steam locomotive power in America. Introduction. Detailed captions. xi+ 129pp. 9 x 12.   27393-8

AMERICA'S LIGHTHOUSES: An Illustrated History, Francis Ross Holland, Jr. Delightfully written, profusely illustrated fact-filled survey of over 200 American lighthouses since 1716. History, anecdotes, technological advances, more. 240pp. 8 x 10¾.
                                                                                      25576-X

TOWARDS A NEW ARCHITECTURE, Le Corbusier. Pioneering manifesto by founder of "International School." Technical and aesthetic theories, views of industry, economics, relation of form to function, "mass-production split" and much more. Profusely illustrated. 320pp. 6⅛ x 9¼. (Available in U.S. only.)   25023-7

HOW THE OTHER HALF LIVES, Jacob Riis. Famous journalistic record, exposing poverty and degradation of New York slums around 1900, by major social reformer. 100 striking and influential photographs. 233pp. 10 x 7⅞.   22012-5

FRUIT KEY AND TWIG KEY TO TREES AND SHRUBS, William M. Harlow. One of the handiest and most widely used identification aids. Fruit key covers 120 deciduous and evergreen species; twig key 160 deciduous species. Easily used. Over 300 photographs. 126pp. 5⅜ x 8½.   20511-8

COMMON BIRD SONGS, Dr. Donald J. Borror. Songs of 60 most common U.S. birds: robins, sparrows, cardinals, bluejays, finches, more—arranged in order of increasing complexity. Up to 9 variations of songs of each species.
                                                                 Cassette and manual 99911-4

ORCHIDS AS HOUSE PLANTS, Rebecca Tyson Northen. Grow cattleyas and many other kinds of orchids—in a window, in a case, or under artificial light. 63 illustrations. 148pp. 5⅜ x 8½.   23261-1

MONSTER MAZES, Dave Phillips. Masterful mazes at four levels of difficulty. Avoid deadly perils and evil creatures to find magical treasures. Solutions for all 32 exciting illustrated puzzles. 48pp. 8¼ x 11.   26005-4

MOZART'S DON GIOVANNI (DOVER OPERA LIBRETTO SERIES), Wolfgang Amadeus Mozart. Introduced and translated by Ellen H. Bleiler. Standard Italian libretto, with complete English translation. Convenient and thoroughly portable—an ideal companion for reading along with a recording or the performance itself. Introduction. List of characters. Plot summary. 121pp. 5¼ x 8½.   24944-1

TECHNICAL MANUAL AND DICTIONARY OF CLASSICAL BALLET, Gail Grant. Defines, explains, comments on steps, movements, poses and concepts. 15-page pictorial section. Basic book for student, viewer. 127pp. 5⅜ x 8½.   21843-0

THE CLARINET AND CLARINET PLAYING, David Pino. Lively, comprehensive work features suggestions about technique, musicianship, and musical interpretation, as well as guidelines for teaching, making your own reeds, and preparing for public performance. Includes an intriguing look at clarinet history. "A godsend," *The Clarinet,* Journal of the International Clarinet Society. Appendixes. 7 illus. 320pp. 5⅜ x 8½. 40270-3

HOLLYWOOD GLAMOR PORTRAITS, John Kobal (ed.). 145 photos from 1926-49. Harlow, Gable, Bogart, Bacall; 94 stars in all. Full background on photographers, technical aspects. 160pp. 8⅜ x 11¼. 23352-9

THE ANNOTATED CASEY AT THE BAT: A Collection of Ballads about the Mighty Casey/Third, Revised Edition, Martin Gardner (ed.). Amusing sequels and parodies of one of America's best-loved poems: Casey's Revenge, Why Casey Whiffed, Casey's Sister at the Bat, others. 256pp. 5⅜ x 8½. 28598-7

THE RAVEN AND OTHER FAVORITE POEMS, Edgar Allan Poe. Over 40 of the author's most memorable poems: "The Bells," "Ulalume," "Israfel," "To Helen," "The Conqueror Worm," "Eldorado," "Annabel Lee," many more. Alphabetic lists of titles and first lines. 64pp. 5³⁄₁₆ x 8¼. 26685-0

PERSONAL MEMOIRS OF U. S. GRANT, Ulysses Simpson Grant. Intelligent, deeply moving firsthand account of Civil War campaigns, considered by many the finest military memoirs ever written. Includes letters, historic photographs, maps and more. 528pp. 6⅛ x 9¼. 28587-1

ANCIENT EGYPTIAN MATERIALS AND INDUSTRIES, A. Lucas and J. Harris. Fascinating, comprehensive, thoroughly documented text describes this ancient civilization's vast resources and the processes that incorporated them in daily life, including the use of animal products, building materials, cosmetics, perfumes and incense, fibers, glazed ware, glass and its manufacture, materials used in the mummification process, and much more. 544pp. 6⅛ x 9¼. (Available in U.S. only.) 40446-3

RUSSIAN STORIES/RUSSKIE RASSKAZY: A Dual-Language Book, edited by Gleb Struve. Twelve tales by such masters as Chekhov, Tolstoy, Dostoevsky, Pushkin, others. Excellent word-for-word English translations on facing pages, plus teaching and study aids, Russian/English vocabulary, biographical/critical introductions, more. 416pp. 5⅜ x 8½. 26244-8

PHILADELPHIA THEN AND NOW: 60 Sites Photographed in the Past and Present, Kenneth Finkel and Susan Oyama. Rare photographs of City Hall, Logan Square, Independence Hall, Betsy Ross House, other landmarks juxtaposed with contemporary views. Captures changing face of historic city. Introduction. Captions. 128pp. 8¼ x 11. 25790-8

AIA ARCHITECTURAL GUIDE TO NASSAU AND SUFFOLK COUNTIES, LONG ISLAND, The American Institute of Architects, Long Island Chapter, and the Society for the Preservation of Long Island Antiquities. Comprehensive, well-researched and generously illustrated volume brings to life over three centuries of Long Island's great architectural heritage. More than 240 photographs with authoritative, extensively detailed captions. 176pp. 8¼ x 11. 26946-9

NORTH AMERICAN INDIAN LIFE: Customs and Traditions of 23 Tribes, Elsie Clews Parsons (ed.). 27 fictionalized essays by noted anthropologists examine religion, customs, government, additional facets of life among the Winnebago, Crow, Zuni, Eskimo, other tribes. 480pp. 6⅛ x 9¼. 27377-6

FRANK LLOYD WRIGHT'S DANA HOUSE, Donald Hoffmann. Pictorial essay of residential masterpiece with over 160 interior and exterior photos, plans, elevations, sketches and studies. 128pp. 9¼ x 10¾. 29120-0

THE MALE AND FEMALE FIGURE IN MOTION: 60 Classic Photographic Sequences, Eadweard Muybridge. 60 true-action photographs of men and women walking, running, climbing, bending, turning, etc., reproduced from rare 19th-century masterpiece. vi + 121pp. 9 x 12. 24745-7

1001 QUESTIONS ANSWERED ABOUT THE SEASHORE, N. J. Berrill and Jacquelyn Berrill. Queries answered about dolphins, sea snails, sponges, starfish, fishes, shore birds, many others. Covers appearance, breeding, growth, feeding, much more. 305pp. 5¼ x 8¼. 23366-9

ATTRACTING BIRDS TO YOUR YARD, William J. Weber. Easy-to-follow guide offers advice on how to attract the greatest diversity of birds: birdhouses, feeders, water and waterers, much more. 96pp. 5³⁄₁₆ x 8¼. 28927-3

MEDICINAL AND OTHER USES OF NORTH AMERICAN PLANTS: A Historical Survey with Special Reference to the Eastern Indian Tribes, Charlotte Erichsen-Brown. Chronological historical citations document 500 years of usage of plants, trees, shrubs native to eastern Canada, northeastern U.S. Also complete identifying information. 343 illustrations. 544pp. 6½ x 9¼. 25951-X

STORYBOOK MAZES, Dave Phillips. 23 stories and mazes on two-page spreads: Wizard of Oz, Treasure Island, Robin Hood, etc. Solutions. 64pp. 8¼ x 11. 23628-5

AMERICAN NEGRO SONGS: 230 Folk Songs and Spirituals, Religious and Secular, John W. Work. This authoritative study traces the African influences of songs sung and played by black Americans at work, in church, and as entertainment. The author discusses the lyric significance of such songs as "Swing Low, Sweet Chariot," "John Henry," and others and offers the words and music for 230 songs. Bibliography. Index of Song Titles. 272pp. 6½ x 9¼. 40271-1

MOVIE-STAR PORTRAITS OF THE FORTIES, John Kobal (ed.). 163 glamor, studio photos of 106 stars of the 1940s: Rita Hayworth, Ava Gardner, Marlon Brando, Clark Gable, many more. 176pp. 8⅜ x 11¼. 23546-7

BENCHLEY LOST AND FOUND, Robert Benchley. Finest humor from early 30s, about pet peeves, child psychologists, post office and others. Mostly unavailable elsewhere. 73 illustrations by Peter Arno and others. 183pp. 5⅜ x 8½. 22410-4

YEKL and THE IMPORTED BRIDEGROOM AND OTHER STORIES OF YIDDISH NEW YORK, Abraham Cahan. Film Hester Street based on *Yekl* (1896). Novel, other stories among first about Jewish immigrants on N.Y.'s East Side. 240pp. 5⅜ x 8½. 22427-9

SELECTED POEMS, Walt Whitman. Generous sampling from *Leaves of Grass*. Twenty-four poems include "I Hear America Singing," "Song of the Open Road," "I Sing the Body Electric," "When Lilacs Last in the Dooryard Bloom'd," "O Captain! My Captain!"–all reprinted from an authoritative edition. Lists of titles and first lines. 128pp. 5³⁄₁₆ x 8¼. 26878-0

THE BEST TALES OF HOFFMANN, E. T. A. Hoffmann. 10 of Hoffmann's most important stories: "Nutcracker and the King of Mice," "The Golden Flowerpot," etc. 458pp. 5⅜ x 8½. 21793-0

FROM FETISH TO GOD IN ANCIENT EGYPT, E. A. Wallis Budge. Rich detailed survey of Egyptian conception of "God" and gods, magic, cult of animals, Osiris, more. Also, superb English translations of hymns and legends. 240 illustrations. 545pp. 5⅜ x 8½. 25803-3

FRENCH STORIES/CONTES FRANÇAIS: A Dual-Language Book, Wallace Fowlie. Ten stories by French masters, Voltaire to Camus: "Micromegas" by Voltaire; "The Atheist's Mass" by Balzac; "Minuet" by de Maupassant; "The Guest" by Camus, six more. Excellent English translations on facing pages. Also French-English vocabulary list, exercises, more. 352pp. 5⅜ x 8½. 26443-2

CHICAGO AT THE TURN OF THE CENTURY IN PHOTOGRAPHS: 122 Historic Views from the Collections of the Chicago Historical Society, Larry A. Viskochil. Rare large-format prints offer detailed views of City Hall, State Street, the Loop, Hull House, Union Station, many other landmarks, circa 1904-1913. Introduction. Captions. Maps. 144pp. 9⅜ x 12¼. 24656-6

OLD BROOKLYN IN EARLY PHOTOGRAPHS, 1865-1929, William Lee Younger. Luna Park, Gravesend race track, construction of Grand Army Plaza, moving of Hotel Brighton, etc. 157 previously unpublished photographs. 165pp. 8⅞ x 11¾. 23587-4

THE MYTHS OF THE NORTH AMERICAN INDIANS, Lewis Spence. Rich anthology of the myths and legends of the Algonquins, Iroquois, Pawnees and Sioux, prefaced by an extensive historical and ethnological commentary. 36 illustrations. 480pp. 5⅜ x 8½. 25967-6

AN ENCYCLOPEDIA OF BATTLES: Accounts of Over 1,560 Battles from 1479 B.C. to the Present, David Eggenberger. Essential details of every major battle in recorded history from the first battle of Megiddo in 1479 B.C. to Grenada in 1984. List of Battle Maps. New Appendix covering the years 1967-1984. Index. 99 illustrations. 544pp. 6½ x 9¼. 24913-1

SAILING ALONE AROUND THE WORLD, Captain Joshua Slocum. First man to sail around the world, alone, in small boat. One of great feats of seamanship told in delightful manner. 67 illustrations. 294pp. 5⅜ x 8½. 20326-3

ANARCHISM AND OTHER ESSAYS, Emma Goldman. Powerful, penetrating, prophetic essays on direct action, role of minorities, prison reform, puritan hypocrisy, violence, etc. 271pp. 5⅜ x 8½. 22484-8

MYTHS OF THE HINDUS AND BUDDHISTS, Ananda K. Coomaraswamy and Sister Nivedita. Great stories of the epics; deeds of Krishna, Shiva, taken from puranas, Vedas, folk tales; etc. 32 illustrations. 400pp. 5⅜ x 8½. 21759-0

THE TRAUMA OF BIRTH, Otto Rank. Rank's controversial thesis that anxiety neurosis is caused by profound psychological trauma which occurs at birth. 256pp. 5⅜ x 8½. 27974-X

A THEOLOGICO-POLITICAL TREATISE, Benedict Spinoza. Also contains unfinished Political Treatise. Great classic on religious liberty, theory of government on common consent. R. Elwes translation. Total of 421pp. 5⅜ x 8½. 20249-6

MY BONDAGE AND MY FREEDOM, Frederick Douglass. Born a slave, Douglass became outspoken force in antislavery movement. The best of Douglass' autobiographies. Graphic description of slave life. 464pp. 5⅜ x 8½.   22457-0

FOLLOWING THE EQUATOR: A Journey Around the World, Mark Twain. Fascinating humorous account of 1897 voyage to Hawaii, Australia, India, New Zealand, etc. Ironic, bemused reports on peoples, customs, climate, flora and fauna, politics, much more. 197 illustrations. 720pp. 5⅜ x 8½.   26113-1

THE PEOPLE CALLED SHAKERS, Edward D. Andrews. Definitive study of Shakers: origins, beliefs, practices, dances, social organization, furniture and crafts, etc. 33 illustrations. 351pp. 5⅜ x 8½.   21081-2

THE MYTHS OF GREECE AND ROME, H. A. Guerber. A classic of mythology, generously illustrated, long prized for its simple, graphic, accurate retelling of the principal myths of Greece and Rome, and for its commentary on their origins and significance. With 64 illustrations by Michelangelo, Raphael, Titian, Rubens, Canova, Bernini and others. 480pp. 5⅜ x 8½.   27584-1

PSYCHOLOGY OF MUSIC, Carl E. Seashore. Classic work discusses music as a medium from psychological viewpoint. Clear treatment of physical acoustics, auditory apparatus, sound perception, development of musical skills, nature of musical feeling, host of other topics. 88 figures. 408pp. 5⅜ x 8½.   21851-1

THE PHILOSOPHY OF HISTORY, Georg W. Hegel. Great classic of Western thought develops concept that history is not chance but rational process, the evolution of freedom. 457pp. 5⅜ x 8½.   20112-0

THE BOOK OF TEA, Kakuzo Okakura. Minor classic of the Orient: entertaining, charming explanation, interpretation of traditional Japanese culture in terms of tea ceremony. 94pp. 5⅜ x 8½.   20070-1

LIFE IN ANCIENT EGYPT, Adolf Erman. Fullest, most thorough, detailed older account with much not in more recent books, domestic life, religion, magic, medicine, commerce, much more. Many illustrations reproduce tomb paintings, carvings, hieroglyphs, etc. 597pp. 5⅜ x 8½.   22632-8

SUNDIALS, Their Theory and Construction, Albert Waugh. Far and away the best, most thorough coverage of ideas, mathematics concerned, types, construction, adjusting anywhere. Simple, nontechnical treatment allows even children to build several of these dials. Over 100 illustrations. 230pp. 5⅜ x 8½.   22947-5

THEORETICAL HYDRODYNAMICS, L. M. Milne-Thomson. Classic exposition of the mathematical theory of fluid motion, applicable to both hydrodynamics and aerodynamics. Over 600 exercises. 768pp. 6⅛ x 9¼.   68970-0

SONGS OF EXPERIENCE: Facsimile Reproduction with 26 Plates in Full Color, William Blake. 26 full-color plates from a rare 1826 edition. Includes "The Tyger," "London," "Holy Thursday," and other poems. Printed text of poems. 48pp. 5¼ x 7.
                24636-1

OLD-TIME VIGNETTES IN FULL COLOR, Carol Belanger Grafton (ed.). Over 390 charming, often sentimental illustrations, selected from archives of Victorian graphics–pretty women posing, children playing, food, flowers, kittens and puppies, smiling cherubs, birds and butterflies, much more. All copyright-free. 48pp. 9¼ x 12¼.
                27269-9

PERSPECTIVE FOR ARTISTS, Rex Vicat Cole. Depth, perspective of sky and sea, shadows, much more, not usually covered. 391 diagrams, 81 reproductions of drawings and paintings. 279pp. 5⅜ x 8½. 22487-2

DRAWING THE LIVING FIGURE, Joseph Sheppard. Innovative approach to artistic anatomy focuses on specifics of surface anatomy, rather than muscles and bones. Over 170 drawings of live models in front, back and side views, and in widely varying poses. Accompanying diagrams. 177 illustrations. Introduction. Index. 144pp. 8⅜ x11¼. 26723-7

GOTHIC AND OLD ENGLISH ALPHABETS: 100 Complete Fonts, Dan X. Solo. Add power, elegance to posters, signs, other graphics with 100 stunning copyright-free alphabets: Blackstone, Dolbey, Germania, 97 more–including many lower-case, numerals, punctuation marks. 104pp. 8⅛ x 11. 24695-7

HOW TO DO BEADWORK, Mary White. Fundamental book on craft from simple projects to five-bead chains and woven works. 106 illustrations. 142pp. 5⅜ x 8. 20697-1

THE BOOK OF WOOD CARVING, Charles Marshall Sayers. Finest book for beginners discusses fundamentals and offers 34 designs. "Absolutely first rate . . . well thought out and well executed."–E. J. Tangerman. 118pp. 7¾ x 10⅝. 23654-4

ILLUSTRATED CATALOG OF CIVIL WAR MILITARY GOODS: Union Army Weapons, Insignia, Uniform Accessories, and Other Equipment, Schuyler, Hartley, and Graham. Rare, profusely illustrated 1846 catalog includes Union Army uniform and dress regulations, arms and ammunition, coats, insignia, flags, swords, rifles, etc. 226 illustrations. 160pp. 9 x 12. 24939-5

WOMEN'S FASHIONS OF THE EARLY 1900s: An Unabridged Republication of "New York Fashions, 1909," National Cloak & Suit Co. Rare catalog of mail-order fashions documents women's and children's clothing styles shortly after the turn of the century. Captions offer full descriptions, prices. Invaluable resource for fashion, costume historians. Approximately 725 illustrations. 128pp. 8⅜ x 11¼. 27276-1

THE 1912 AND 1915 GUSTAV STICKLEY FURNITURE CATALOGS, Gustav Stickley. With over 200 detailed illustrations and descriptions, these two catalogs are essential reading and reference materials and identification guides for Stickley furniture. Captions cite materials, dimensions and prices. 112pp. 6½ x 9¼. 26676-1

EARLY AMERICAN LOCOMOTIVES, John H. White, Jr. Finest locomotive engravings from early 19th century: historical (1804–74), main-line (after 1870), special, foreign, etc. 147 plates. 142pp. 11⅜ x 8¼. 22772-3

THE TALL SHIPS OF TODAY IN PHOTOGRAPHS, Frank O. Braynard. Lavishly illustrated tribute to nearly 100 majestic contemporary sailing vessels: Amerigo Vespucci, Clearwater, Constitution, Eagle, Mayflower, Sea Cloud, Victory, many more. Authoritative captions provide statistics, background on each ship. 190 black-and-white photographs and illustrations. Introduction. 128pp. 8⅞ x 11¾. 27163-3

LITTLE BOOK OF EARLY AMERICAN CRAFTS AND TRADES, Peter Stockham (ed.). 1807 children's book explains crafts and trades: baker, hatter, cooper, potter, and many others. 23 copperplate illustrations. 140pp. 4⅝ x 6.   23336-7

VICTORIAN FASHIONS AND COSTUMES FROM HARPER'S BAZAR, 1867–1898, Stella Blum (ed.). Day costumes, evening wear, sports clothes, shoes, hats, other accessories in over 1,000 detailed engravings. 320pp. 9⅜ x 12¼. 22990-4

GUSTAV STICKLEY, THE CRAFTSMAN, Mary Ann Smith. Superb study surveys broad scope of Stickley's achievement, especially in architecture. Design philosophy, rise and fall of the Craftsman empire, descriptions and floor plans for many Craftsman houses, more. 86 black-and-white halftones. 31 line illustrations. Introduction 208pp. 6½ x 9¼.   27210-9

THE LONG ISLAND RAIL ROAD IN EARLY PHOTOGRAPHS, Ron Ziel. Over 220 rare photos, informative text document origin (1844) and development of rail service on Long Island. Vintage views of early trains, locomotives, stations, passengers, crews, much more. Captions. 8⅞ x 11¾.   26301-0

VOYAGE OF THE LIBERDADE, Joshua Slocum. Great 19th-century mariner's thrilling, first-hand account of the wreck of his ship off South America, the 35-foot boat he built from the wreckage, and its remarkable voyage home. 128pp. 5⅜ x 8½.
40022-0

TEN BOOKS ON ARCHITECTURE, Vitruvius. The most important book ever written on architecture. Early Roman aesthetics, technology, classical orders, site selection, all other aspects. Morgan translation. 331pp. 5⅜ x 8½.   20645-9

THE HUMAN FIGURE IN MOTION, Eadweard Muybridge. More than 4,500 stopped-action photos, in action series, showing undraped men, women, children jumping, lying down, throwing, sitting, wrestling, carrying, etc. 390pp. 7⅞ x 10⅝.
20204-6 Clothbd.

TREES OF THE EASTERN AND CENTRAL UNITED STATES AND CANADA, William M. Harlow. Best one-volume guide to 140 trees. Full descriptions, woodlore, range, etc. Over 600 illustrations. Handy size. 288pp. 4½ x 6⅜.   20395-6

SONGS OF WESTERN BIRDS, Dr. Donald J. Borror. Complete song and call repertoire of 60 western species, including flycatchers, juncoes, cactus wrens, many more–includes fully illustrated booklet.   Cassette and manual 99913-0

GROWING AND USING HERBS AND SPICES, Milo Miloradovich. Versatile handbook provides all the information needed for cultivation and use of all the herbs and spices available in North America. 4 illustrations. Index. Glossary. 236pp. 5⅜ x 8½.
25058-X

BIG BOOK OF MAZES AND LABYRINTHS, Walter Shepherd. 50 mazes and labyrinths in all–classical, solid, ripple, and more–in one great volume. Perfect inexpensive puzzler for clever youngsters. Full solutions. 112pp. 8⅛ x 11.   22951-3

PIANO TUNING, J. Cree Fischer. Clearest, best book for beginner, amateur. Simple repairs, raising dropped notes, tuning by easy method of flattened fifths. No previous skills needed. 4 illustrations. 201pp. 5⅜ x 8½. 23267-0

HINTS TO SINGERS, Lillian Nordica. Selecting the right teacher, developing confidence, overcoming stage fright, and many other important skills receive thoughtful discussion in this indispensible guide, written by a world-famous diva of four decades' experience. 96pp. 5⅜ x 8½. 40094-8

THE COMPLETE NONSENSE OF EDWARD LEAR, Edward Lear. All nonsense limericks, zany alphabets, Owl and Pussycat, songs, nonsense botany, etc., illustrated by Lear. Total of 320pp. 5⅜ x 8½. (Available in U.S. only.) 20167-8

VICTORIAN PARLOUR POETRY: An Annotated Anthology, Michael R. Turner. 117 gems by Longfellow, Tennyson, Browning, many lesser-known poets. "The Village Blacksmith," "Curfew Must Not Ring Tonight," "Only a Baby Small," dozens more, often difficult to find elsewhere. Index of poets, titles, first lines. xxiii + 325pp. 5⅝ x 8¼. 27044-0

DUBLINERS, James Joyce. Fifteen stories offer vivid, tightly focused observations of the lives of Dublin's poorer classes. At least one, "The Dead," is considered a masterpiece. Reprinted complete and unabridged from standard edition. 160pp. 5³⁄₁₆ x 8¼. 26870-5

GREAT WEIRD TALES: 14 Stories by Lovecraft, Blackwood, Machen and Others, S. T. Joshi (ed.). 14 spellbinding tales, including "The Sin Eater," by Fiona McLeod, "The Eye Above the Mantel," by Frank Belknap Long, as well as renowned works by R. H. Barlow, Lord Dunsany, Arthur Machen, W. C. Morrow and eight other masters of the genre. 256pp. 5⅜ x 8½. (Available in U.S. only.) 40436-6

THE BOOK OF THE SACRED MAGIC OF ABRAMELIN THE MAGE, translated by S. MacGregor Mathers. Medieval manuscript of ceremonial magic. Basic document in Aleister Crowley, Golden Dawn groups. 268pp. 5⅜ x 8½. 23211-5

NEW RUSSIAN-ENGLISH AND ENGLISH-RUSSIAN DICTIONARY, M. A. O'Brien. This is a remarkably handy Russian dictionary, containing a surprising amount of information, including over 70,000 entries. 366pp. 4½ x 6⅛. 20208-9

HISTORIC HOMES OF THE AMERICAN PRESIDENTS, Second, Revised Edition, Irvin Haas. A traveler's guide to American Presidential homes, most open to the public, depicting and describing homes occupied by every American President from George Washington to George Bush. With visiting hours, admission charges, travel routes. 175 photographs. Index. 160pp. 8¼ x 11. 26751-2

NEW YORK IN THE FORTIES, Andreas Feininger. 162 brilliant photographs by the well-known photographer, formerly with *Life* magazine. Commuters, shoppers, Times Square at night, much else from city at its peak. Captions by John von Hartz. 181pp. 9¼ x 10¾. 23585-8

INDIAN SIGN LANGUAGE, William Tomkins. Over 525 signs developed by Sioux and other tribes. Written instructions and diagrams. Also 290 pictographs. 111pp. 6⅛ x 9¼. 22029-X

ANATOMY: A Complete Guide for Artists, Joseph Sheppard. A master of figure drawing shows artists how to render human anatomy convincingly. Over 460 illustrations. 224pp. 8⅜ x 11¼. 27279-6

MEDIEVAL CALLIGRAPHY: Its History and Technique, Marc Drogin. Spirited history, comprehensive instruction manual covers 13 styles (ca. 4th century through 15th). Excellent photographs; directions for duplicating medieval techniques with modern tools. 224pp. 8⅜ x 11¼. 26142-5

DRIED FLOWERS: How to Prepare Them, Sarah Whitlock and Martha Rankin. Complete instructions on how to use silica gel, meal and borax, perlite aggregate, sand and borax, glycerine and water to create attractive permanent flower arrangements. 12 illustrations. 32pp. 5⅜ x 8½. 21802-3

EASY-TO-MAKE BIRD FEEDERS FOR WOODWORKERS, Scott D. Campbell. Detailed, simple-to-use guide for designing, constructing, caring for and using feeders. Text, illustrations for 12 classic and contemporary designs. 96pp. 5⅜ x 8½.
25847-5

SCOTTISH WONDER TALES FROM MYTH AND LEGEND, Donald A. Mackenzie. 16 lively tales tell of giants rumbling down mountainsides, of a magic wand that turns stone pillars into warriors, of gods and goddesses, evil hags, powerful forces and more. 240pp. 5⅜ x 8½. 29677-6

THE HISTORY OF UNDERCLOTHES, C. Willett Cunnington and Phyllis Cunnington. Fascinating, well-documented survey covering six centuries of English undergarments, enhanced with over 100 illustrations: 12th-century laced-up bodice, footed long drawers (1795), 19th-century bustles, l9th-century corsets for men, Victorian "bust improvers," much more. 272pp. 5⅜ x 8¼. 27124-2

ARTS AND CRAFTS FURNITURE: The Complete Brooks Catalog of 1912, Brooks Manufacturing Co. Photos and detailed descriptions of more than 150 now very collectible furniture designs from the Arts and Crafts movement depict davenports, settees, buffets, desks, tables, chairs, bedsteads, dressers and more, all built of solid, quarter-sawed oak. Invaluable for students and enthusiasts of antiques, Americana and the decorative arts. 80pp. 6½ x 9¼. 27471-3

WILBUR AND ORVILLE: A Biography of the Wright Brothers, Fred Howard. Definitive, crisply written study tells the full story of the brothers' lives and work. A vividly written biography, unparalleled in scope and color, that also captures the spirit of an extraordinary era. 560pp. 6⅛ x 9¼. 40297-5

THE ARTS OF THE SAILOR: Knotting, Splicing and Ropework, Hervey Garrett Smith. Indispensable shipboard reference covers tools, basic knots and useful hitches; handsewing and canvas work, more. Over 100 illustrations. Delightful reading for sea lovers. 256pp. 5⅜ x 8½. 26440-8

FRANK LLOYD WRIGHT'S FALLINGWATER: The House and Its History, Second, Revised Edition, Donald Hoffmann. A total revision–both in text and illustrations–of the standard document on Fallingwater, the boldest, most personal architectural statement of Wright's mature years, updated with valuable new material from the recently opened Frank Lloyd Wright Archives. "Fascinating"–*The New York Times*. 116 illustrations. 128pp. 9¼ x 10¾. 27430-6

PHOTOGRAPHIC SKETCHBOOK OF THE CIVIL WAR, Alexander Gardner. 100 photos taken on field during the Civil War. Famous shots of Manassas Harper's Ferry, Lincoln, Richmond, slave pens, etc. 244pp. 10⅝ x 8¼. 22731-6

FIVE ACRES AND INDEPENDENCE, Maurice G. Kains. Great back-to-the-land classic explains basics of self-sufficient farming. The one book to get. 95 illustrations. 397pp. 5⅜ x 8½. 20974-1

SONGS OF EASTERN BIRDS, Dr. Donald J. Borror. Songs and calls of 60 species most common to eastern U.S.: warblers, woodpeckers, flycatchers, thrushes, larks, many more in high-quality recording. Cassette and manual 99912-2

A MODERN HERBAL, Margaret Grieve. Much the fullest, most exact, most useful compilation of herbal material. Gigantic alphabetical encyclopedia, from aconite to zedoary, gives botanical information, medical properties, folklore, economic uses, much else. Indispensable to serious reader. 161 illustrations. 888pp. 6½ x 9¼. 2-vol. set. (Available in U.S. only.) Vol. I: 22798-7
Vol. II: 22799-5

HIDDEN TREASURE MAZE BOOK, Dave Phillips. Solve 34 challenging mazes accompanied by heroic tales of adventure. Evil dragons, people-eating plants, blood-thirsty giants, many more dangerous adversaries lurk at every twist and turn. 34 mazes, stories, solutions. 48pp. 8¼ x 11. 24566-7

LETTERS OF W. A. MOZART, Wolfgang A. Mozart. Remarkable letters show bawdy wit, humor, imagination, musical insights, contemporary musical world; includes some letters from Leopold Mozart. 276pp. 5⅜ x 8½. 22859-2

BASIC PRINCIPLES OF CLASSICAL BALLET, Agrippina Vaganova. Great Russian theoretician, teacher explains methods for teaching classical ballet. 118 illustrations. 175pp. 5⅜ x 8½. 22036-2

THE JUMPING FROG, Mark Twain. Revenge edition. The original story of The Celebrated Jumping Frog of Calaveras County, a hapless French translation, and Twain's hilarious "retranslation" from the French. 12 illustrations. 66pp. 5⅜ x 8½. 22686-7

BEST REMEMBERED POEMS, Martin Gardner (ed.). The 126 poems in this superb collection of 19th- and 20th-century British and American verse range from Shelley's "To a Skylark" to the impassioned "Renascence" of Edna St. Vincent Millay and to Edward Lear's whimsical "The Owl and the Pussycat." 224pp. 5⅜ x 8½. 27165-X

COMPLETE SONNETS, William Shakespeare. Over 150 exquisite poems deal with love, friendship, the tyranny of time, beauty's evanescence, death and other themes in language of remarkable power, precision and beauty. Glossary of archaic terms. 80pp. 5³⁄₁₆ x 8¼. 26686-9

THE BATTLES THAT CHANGED HISTORY, Fletcher Pratt. Eminent historian profiles 16 crucial conflicts, ancient to modern, that changed the course of civilization. 352pp. 5⅜ x 8½. 41129-X

THE WIT AND HUMOR OF OSCAR WILDE, Alvin Redman (ed.). More than 1,000 ripostes, paradoxes, wisecracks: Work is the curse of the drinking classes; I can resist everything except temptation; etc. 258pp. 5⅜ x 8½. 20602-5

SHAKESPEARE LEXICON AND QUOTATION DICTIONARY, Alexander Schmidt. Full definitions, locations, shades of meaning in every word in plays and poems. More than 50,000 exact quotations. 1,485pp. 6½ x 9¼. 2-vol. set.
Vol. 1: 22726-X
Vol. 2: 22727-8

SELECTED POEMS, Emily Dickinson. Over 100 best-known, best-loved poems by one of America's foremost poets, reprinted from authoritative early editions. No comparable edition at this price. Index of first lines. 64pp. 5³⁄₁₆ x 8¼. 26466-1

THE INSIDIOUS DR. FU-MANCHU, Sax Rohmer. The first of the popular mystery series introduces a pair of English detectives to their archnemesis, the diabolical Dr. Fu-Manchu. Flavorful atmosphere, fast-paced action, and colorful characters enliven this classic of the genre. 208pp. 5³⁄₁₆ x 8¼. 29898-1

THE MALLEUS MALEFICARUM OF KRAMER AND SPRENGER, translated by Montague Summers. Full text of most important witchhunter's "bible," used by both Catholics and Protestants. 278pp. 6⅝ x 10. 22802-9

SPANISH STORIES/CUENTOS ESPAÑOLES: A Dual-Language Book, Angel Flores (ed.). Unique format offers 13 great stories in Spanish by Cervantes, Borges, others. Faithful English translations on facing pages. 352pp. 5⅜ x 8½. 25399-6

GARDEN CITY, LONG ISLAND, IN EARLY PHOTOGRAPHS, 1869–1919, Mildred H. Smith. Handsome treasury of 118 vintage pictures, accompanied by carefully researched captions, document the Garden City Hotel fire (1899), the Vanderbilt Cup Race (1908), the first airmail flight departing from the Nassau Boulevard Aerodrome (1911), and much more. 96pp. 8⅞ x 11¾. 40669-5

OLD QUEENS, N.Y., IN EARLY PHOTOGRAPHS, Vincent F. Seyfried and William Asadorian. Over 160 rare photographs of Maspeth, Jamaica, Jackson Heights, and other areas. Vintage views of DeWitt Clinton mansion, 1939 World's Fair and more. Captions. 192pp. 8⅞ x 11. 26358-4

CAPTURED BY THE INDIANS: 15 Firsthand Accounts, 1750-1870, Frederick Drimmer. Astounding true historical accounts of grisly torture, bloody conflicts, relentless pursuits, miraculous escapes and more, by people who lived to tell the tale. 384pp. 5⅜ x 8½. 24901-8

THE WORLD'S GREAT SPEECHES (Fourth Enlarged Edition), Lewis Copeland, Lawrence W. Lamm, and Stephen J. McKenna. Nearly 300 speeches provide public speakers with a wealth of updated quotes and inspiration–from Pericles' funeral oration and William Jennings Bryan's "Cross of Gold Speech" to Malcolm X's powerful words on the Black Revolution and Earl of Spenser's tribute to his sister, Diana, Princess of Wales. 944pp. 5⅜ x 8⅜. 40903-1

THE BOOK OF THE SWORD, Sir Richard F. Burton. Great Victorian scholar/adventurer's eloquent, erudite history of the "queen of weapons"–from prehistory to early Roman Empire. Evolution and development of early swords, variations (sabre, broadsword, cutlass, scimitar, etc.), much more. 336pp. 6⅛ x 9¼.
25434-8

AUTOBIOGRAPHY: The Story of My Experiments with Truth, Mohandas K. Gandhi. Boyhood, legal studies, purification, the growth of the Satyagraha (nonviolent protest) movement. Critical, inspiring work of the man responsible for the freedom of India. 480pp. 5⅜ x 8½. (Available in U.S. only.) 24593-4

CELTIC MYTHS AND LEGENDS, T. W. Rolleston. Masterful retelling of Irish and Welsh stories and tales. Cuchulain, King Arthur, Deirdre, the Grail, many more. First paperback edition. 58 full-page illustrations. 512pp. 5⅜ x 8½. 26507-2

THE PRINCIPLES OF PSYCHOLOGY, William James. Famous long course complete, unabridged. Stream of thought, time perception, memory, experimental methods; great work decades ahead of its time. 94 figures. 1,391pp. 5⅜ x 8½. 2-vol. set.
Vol. I: 20381-6 Vol. II: 20382-4

THE WORLD AS WILL AND REPRESENTATION, Arthur Schopenhauer. Definitive English translation of Schopenhauer's life work, correcting more than 1,000 errors, omissions in earlier translations. Translated by E. F. J. Payne. Total of 1,269pp. 5⅜ x 8½. 2-vol. set. Vol. 1: 21761-2 Vol. 2: 21762-0

MAGIC AND MYSTERY IN TIBET, Madame Alexandra David-Neel. Experiences among lamas, magicians, sages, sorcerers, Bonpa wizards. A true psychic discovery. 32 illustrations. 321pp. 5⅜ x 8½. (Available in U.S. only.) 22682-4

THE EGYPTIAN BOOK OF THE DEAD, E. A. Wallis Budge. Complete reproduction of Ani's papyrus, finest ever found. Full hieroglyphic text, interlinear transliteration, word-for-word translation, smooth translation. 533pp. 6½ x 9¼. 21866-X

MATHEMATICS FOR THE NONMATHEMATICIAN, Morris Kline. Detailed, college-level treatment of mathematics in cultural and historical context, with numerous exercises. Recommended Reading Lists. Tables. Numerous figures. 641pp. 5⅜ x 8½. 24823-2

PROBABILISTIC METHODS IN THE THEORY OF STRUCTURES, Isaac Elishakoff. Well-written introduction covers the elements of the theory of probability from two or more random variables, the reliability of such multivariable structures, the theory of random function, Monte Carlo methods of treating problems incapable of exact solution, and more. Examples. 502pp. 5⅜ x 8½. 40691-1

THE RIME OF THE ANCIENT MARINER, Gustave Doré, S. T. Coleridge. Doré's finest work; 34 plates capture moods, subtleties of poem. Flawless full-size reproductions printed on facing pages with authoritative text of poem. "Beautiful. Simply beautiful."–*Publisher's Weekly.* 77pp. 9¼ x 12. 22305-1

NORTH AMERICAN INDIAN DESIGNS FOR ARTISTS AND CRAFTSPEOPLE, Eva Wilson. Over 360 authentic copyright-free designs adapted from Navajo blankets, Hopi pottery, Sioux buffalo hides, more. Geometrics, symbolic figures, plant and animal motifs, etc. 128pp. 8⅜ x 11. (Not for sale in the United Kingdom.) 25341-4

SCULPTURE: Principles and Practice, Louis Slobodkin. Step-by-step approach to clay, plaster, metals, stone; classical and modern. 253 drawings, photos. 255pp. 8⅛ x 11. 22960-2

THE INFLUENCE OF SEA POWER UPON HISTORY, 1660–1783, A. T. Mahan. Influential classic of naval history and tactics still used as text in war colleges. First paperback edition. 4 maps. 24 battle plans. 640pp. 5⅜ x 8½. 25509-3

CATALOG OF DOVER BOOKS

THE STORY OF THE TITANIC AS TOLD BY ITS SURVIVORS, Jack Winocour (ed.). What it was really like. Panic, despair, shocking inefficiency, and a little heroism. More thrilling than any fictional account. 26 illustrations. 320pp. 5⅜ x 8½.
20610-6

FAIRY AND FOLK TALES OF THE IRISH PEASANTRY, William Butler Yeats (ed.). Treasury of 64 tales from the twilight world of Celtic myth and legend: "The Soul Cages," "The Kildare Pooka," "King O'Toole and his Goose," many more. Introduction and Notes by W. B. Yeats. 352pp. 5⅜ x 8½.
26941-8

BUDDHIST MAHAYANA TEXTS, E. B. Cowell and others (eds.). Superb, accurate translations of basic documents in Mahayana Buddhism, highly important in history of religions. The Buddha-karita of Asvaghosha, Larger Sukhavativyuha, more. 448pp. 5⅜ x 8½.
25552-2

ONE TWO THREE . . . INFINITY: Facts and Speculations of Science, George Gamow. Great physicist's fascinating, readable overview of contemporary science: number theory, relativity, fourth dimension, entropy, genes, atomic structure, much more. 128 illustrations. Index. 352pp. 5⅜ x 8½.
25664-2

EXPERIMENTATION AND MEASUREMENT, W. J. Youden. Introductory manual explains laws of measurement in simple terms and offers tips for achieving accuracy and minimizing errors. Mathematics of measurement, use of instruments, experimenting with machines. 1994 edition. Foreword. Preface. Introduction. Epilogue. Selected Readings. Glossary. Index. Tables and figures. 128pp. 5⅜ x 8½.   40451-X

DALÍ ON MODERN ART: The Cuckolds of Antiquated Modern Art, Salvador Dalí. Influential painter skewers modern art and its practitioners. Outrageous evaluations of Picasso, Cézanne, Turner, more. 15 renderings of paintings discussed. 44 calligraphic decorations by Dalí. 96pp. 5⅜ x 8½. (Available in U.S. only.)   29220-7

ANTIQUE PLAYING CARDS: A Pictorial History, Henry René D'Allemagne. Over 900 elaborate, decorative images from rare playing cards (14th–20th centuries): Bacchus, death, dancing dogs, hunting scenes, royal coats of arms, players cheating, much more. 96pp. 9¼ x 12¼.
29265-7

MAKING FURNITURE MASTERPIECES: 30 Projects with Measured Drawings, Franklin H. Gottshall. Step-by-step instructions, illustrations for constructing handsome, useful pieces, among them a Sheraton desk, Chippendale chair, Spanish desk, Queen Anne table and a William and Mary dressing mirror. 224pp. 8⅛ x 11¼.
29338-6

THE FOSSIL BOOK: A Record of Prehistoric Life, Patricia V. Rich et al. Profusely illustrated definitive guide covers everything from single-celled organisms and dinosaurs to birds and mammals and the interplay between climate and man. Over 1,500 illustrations. 760pp. 7½ x 10⅛.
29371-8

Paperbound unless otherwise indicated. Available at your book dealer, online at **www.doverpublications.com**, or by writing to Dept. GI, Dover Publications, Inc., 31 East 2nd Street, Mineola, NY 11501. For current price information or for free catalogues (please indicate field of interest), write to Dover Publications or log on to **www.doverpublications.com** and see every Dover book in print. Dover publishes more than 500 books each year on science, elementary and advanced mathematics, biology, music, art, literary history, social sciences, and other areas.